NUJEEN MUSTAFA
WITH CHRISTINA LAMB

NUJEEN

ONE GIRL'S INCREDIBLE JOURNEY FROM WAR-TORN SYRIA IN A WHEELCHAIR

WILLIAM COLLINS

William Collins
An imprint of HarperCollins*Publishers*
1 London Bridge Street
London SE1 9GF
www.WilliamCollinsBooks.com

First published in Great Britain by William Collins in 2016

1

All photographs from the Mustafa family collection
unless otherwise credited

Map by Martin Brown

A catalogue record for this book is
available from the British Library

ISBN 978-0-00-819278-5 (hardback)
ISBN 978-0-00-819282-2 (trade paperback)

Printed and bound in Great Britain by
Clays Ltd, St Ives plc

MIX
Paper from
responsible sources
FSC® C007454

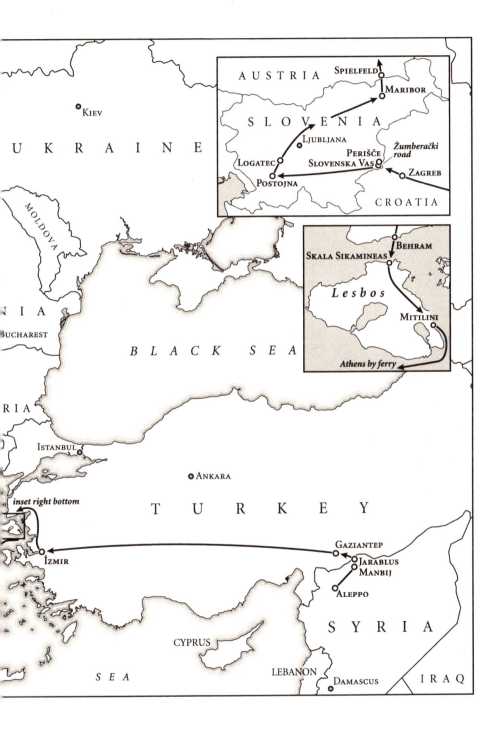

I see Earth! It is so beautiful.

Yuri Gagarin, first man in space, 1961

Contents

NUJEEN

Prologue

The Crossing

Behram, Turkey, 2 September 2015

From the beach we could see the island of Lesbos – and Europe. The sea stretched either side as far as you could see and it was not rough, it was quiet, flecked only by the smallest of white caps that looked as if they were dancing on the waves. The island did not look too far off, rising from the sea like a rocky loaf. But the grey dinghies were small and low in the water, weighed down with as many lives as the smugglers could pack in.

It was the first time I had seen the sea. The first time for everything – travelling on a plane, in a train, leaving my parents, staying in a hotel and now going in a boat! Back in Aleppo I had barely ever left our fifth-floor apartment.

We had heard from those who had gone before that on a fine summer day like this with a working motor a dinghy takes just over an hour to cross the strait. It was one of the shortest routes from Turkey to Greece – just 8 miles. The problem was that the motors were often old and cheap and strained for power with loads of fifty or sixty people, so the trips took three or four hours. On a rainy night when waves reached as high as 10 feet and tossed the boats like toys, sometimes they never made it at all and journeys of hope ended in a watery grave.

The beach was not sandy as I had imagined it would be but pebbly – impossible for my wheelchair. We could see we were in the right place from a ripped cardboard box printed with the words 'Inflatable Rubber Dinghy; Made in China (Max Capacity 15 Pax)', as well as a trail of discarded belongings scattered along the shore like a kind of refugee flotsam and jetsam. There were toothbrushes, nappies and biscuit wrappers, abandoned backpacks and a slew of clothes and shoes. Jeans and T-shirts tossed out because there was no room in the boat and smugglers make you travel as light as possible. A pair of grey high-heeled mules with fluffy black pom-poms, which seemed a crazy thing to have brought on this journey. A child's tiny pink sandal decorated with a plastic rose. A boy's light-up trainers. And a large grey floppy bear with a missing eye that must have been hard for someone to leave behind. All the stuff had turned this beautiful place into a rubbish dump, which made me sad.

We had been in the olive groves all night after being dropped off on the cliff road by the smuggler's mini-bus.

Prologue: The Crossing

From there we had to walk down the hill to the shore which was about a mile. That may not sound much but it feels a very long way in a wheelchair over a rough track with only your sister to push and a fierce Turkish sun beating down and driving sweat into your eyes. There was a road zigzagging down the hill which would have been much easier, but we couldn't walk along that as we might be spotted and arrested by the Turkish gendarmerie who could put us in a detention centre or even send us back.

I was with two of my four elder sisters – Nahda, though she had her baby and three little girls to handle, and my closest sister Nasrine who always looks after me and is as beautiful as her name, which means a white rose that grows on the hills of Kurdistan. Also with us were some cousins whose parents – my aunt and uncle – had been shot dead by Daesh snipers in June when they went to a funeral in Kobane, a day I don't want to think about.

The way was bumpy. Annoyingly, Nasrine pulled the wheelchair so I was facing backwards and only got occasional glimpses of the sea, but when I did it was sparkling blue. Blue is my favourite colour because it's the colour of God's planet. Everyone got very hot and bothered. The chair was too big for me and I gripped the sides so hard that my arms hurt and my bottom got bruised from all the bumping, but I didn't say anything.

As with everywhere we had passed through I told my sisters some local information I had gathered before we left.

I was excited that on top of the hill above us was the ancient town of Assos which had a ruined temple to the goddess Athena and, even better, was where Aristotle once lived. He'd started a school of philosophy overlooking the sea so he could watch the tides and challenge the theory of his former master Plato that tides were turbulence caused by rivers. Then the Persians attacked and made the philosophers flee and Aristotle ended up in Macedonia as tutor to a young Alexander the Great. St Paul the apostle also passed through on his own journey to Lesbos from Syria. As always my sisters didn't seem very interested.

I gave up trying to inform them and watched the seagulls having fun gliding on thermals and making noisy loops high in the blue, blue sky, never once stalling. How I wished I could fly. Even astronauts don't have that freedom.

Nasrine kept checking the Samsung smartphone our brother Mustafa had bought us for the journey to make sure we were following the Google map coordinates given to us by the smuggler. Yet, when we finally got to the shore, it turned out we were not in the right place. Every smuggler has their own 'point' – we had coloured strips of fabric tied round our wrists to identify us – and we were at the wrong one.

Where we needed to be wasn't far along the beach but when we got to the end there was a sheer cliff blocking us off. The only way round was to swim, which we obviously couldn't do. So we'd ended up having to walk up and down another rugged hill to reach the right point on the shore.

Those slopes were like hell. If you slipped and fell into the sea you'd definitely be dead. It was so rocky that I couldn't be pushed or pulled but had to be carried. My cousins teased me, 'You are the Queen, Queen Nujeen!'

By the time we got to the right beach the sun was setting, an explosion of pink and purple as if one of my little nieces was squiggling coloured crayons across the sky. From the hills above I heard the gentle tinkle of goat-bells.

We spent the night in the olive grove. Once the sun had gone the temperature dropped suddenly and the ground was hard and rocky even though Nasrine spread all the clothes we had around me. But I was terribly exhausted, having never spent so much time outside in my life, and I slept most of the night. We couldn't make a fire because it might attract police. Some people used the cardboard dinghy cartons to try and cover themselves. It felt like one of those movies where a group go camping and something terrible happens.

Breakfast was sugar cubes and Nutella which might sound exciting but kind of sucks when it's all you have. The smugglers had promised we would leave early in the morning and by dawn we were all ready on the beach in our life jackets. Our phones were tied inside party balloons to protect them on the crossing, a trick we had been shown how to do in İzmir.

There were several other groups waiting. We had paid $1,500 each instead of the usual $1,000 to have a dinghy just for our family, but it seemed others would be in our boat. We would be thirty-eight in total – twenty-seven adults and eleven children. Now we were here there was nothing we could do – we couldn't go back and people said the smugglers used knives and cattle prods on those who changed their minds.

The sky was cloudless, and close by I could see that the sea wasn't just one colour, the uniform blue of pictures and my imaginings, but bright turquoise next to the shore then a deeper blue darkening to grey then indigo near the island. I knew the sea only from National Geographic documentaries and now it was as if I was part of one. I felt really wired and couldn't understand why everyone was nervous. For me it was like the biggest adventure!

Other kids were running and collecting pebbles of different colours. A small Afghan boy gave me one the shape of a dove, flat and grey with a white marble vein running through it. It was cool to the touch and worn smooth by the sea. It's not always easy for me to hold things in my awkward fingers but I wasn't letting go of that.

There were people from Syria like us as well as from Iraq, Morocco and Afghanistan speaking in a language we didn't understand. Some people swapped stories but most didn't say much. They didn't need to. To be leaving all you knew and had built up in your own country to make this dangerous and uncertain journey, it must be bad.

As morning broke we watched the first boats go out. Two set off more or less straight but two were going in all directions. The boats didn't have pilots – what happened was the smugglers let one of the refugees travel for half price or for free if he drove the boat even though none of them had any experience. 'It's just like riding a motorbike,' they claimed. My uncle Ahmed was going to be driving our boat. I guessed he'd never driven one as we had never been to the sea and his old job was running a mobile-phone shop, but he assured us he knew how.

We'd heard that some refugees gun the motor to get half-way across to Greek waters as fast as possible and they burn out the motor. Sometimes the engines don't have enough fuel. If that happens the Turkish coastguard catch you and bring you back. In Café Sinbad in İzmir we'd met a family from Aleppo who had tried to cross six times. We didn't have money to keep trying.

Around 9 a.m. Uncle Ahmed called the smuggler, but he said we must wait for the coastguard to go. 'We have chosen the wrong smuggler,' said Nasrine. I worried we had been cheated again. We hadn't expected to be here so long and were soon hungry and thirsty which was ironic as there was so much water in front of us. My cousins went to try and find water for me and the children but there was nothing near by.

The day got hotter. Though the smuggler had arrived with dinghies for us and the other groups, he said we couldn't go until the coastguard changed shift. The Moroccan men were half naked and started singing. As the afternoon came, the waves started to get higher, making a slapping sound on the shore. None of us wanted to go at night as we'd heard stories of kind of pirates on jet-skis who board boats in the dark to steal motors and the valuables of refugees.

Finally, around 5 p.m., they said the coastguards were changing guard so we could take advantage and go. I looked again at the sea. A mist was coming down and the cry of the seagulls no longer seemed so joyful. A dark shadow lay over the rocky island. Some call that crossing *rihlat al-moot* or the route of death. It would either deliver us to Europe or swallow us up. For the first time I felt scared.

Back home I often watched a series called *Brain Games* on National Geographic which showed how feelings of fear and panic are controlled by the brain, so I began practising breathing deeply and telling myself over and over that I was strong.

PART ONE

To Lose a Country

Syria, 1999–2014

Before they are numbers, these people are
first and foremost human beings.

Pope Francis, Lesbos, 16 April 2016

1

Foreigners in Our Own Land

I don't collect stamps or coins or football cards – I collect facts. Most of all I like facts about physics and space, particularly string theory. Also about history and dynasties like the Romanovs. And controversial people like Howard Hughes and J. Edgar Hoover.

My brother Mustafa says I only need to hear something once to remember it exactly. I can list you all the Romanovs from the first one Tsar Mikhail to Nicholas II who was murdered by the Bolsheviks along with all his family, even his youngest daughter Anastasia. I can tell you exactly what date Queen Elizabeth II became queen of England – both the day her father died and her coronation – and the dates of both her birthdays, actual and official. I'd like to meet her one day and ask her 'What's it like having Queen Victoria as your great-great-grandmother?' and 'Isn't it odd everyone singing a song about saving you?'

I can also tell you that the only animal not to make a sound is a giraffe because it has no vocal cords. This used to be one of my favourite facts, but then people started calling our dictator Bashar al-Assad the Giraffe because he has a long neck.

Now here is a fact I don't think anyone should like. Did you know that one in every 113 people in the world today are refugees or displaced from their homes? Lots of them are escaping wars like the one that has ravaged our country Syria, or those in Iraq, Afghanistan and Libya. Others are running from terrorist groups in Pakistan and Somalia or from persecution by mullah regimes in Iran and Egypt. Then there are ones fleeing dictatorship in Gambia, forced conscription in Eritrea, and hunger and poverty in countries in Africa I never saw on a map. On TV I keep hearing reporters say that the movement of people from the Middle East, North Africa and Central Asia into Europe is the largest refugee crisis since the Second World War. In 2015 more than 1.2 million came to Europe. I was one of them.

I hate the word refugee more than any word in the English language. In German it is *Flüchtling*, which is just as harsh. What it really means is a second-class citizen with a number scrawled on your hand or printed on a wristband, who everyone wishes would somehow go away. The year 2015 was when I became a fact, a statistic, a number. Much as I like facts, we are not numbers, we are human beings and we all have stories. This is mine.

* * *

My name is Nujeen which means new life, and I guess you can say I was unexpected. My mum and dad already had four boys and four girls, and by the time I came along on New Year's Day 1999, twenty-six years after my eldest brother Shiar, some were already married off and the youngest one Nasrine was nine, so everyone thought the family was complete. My mum almost died giving birth to me and was so weak afterwards it was my eldest sister Jamila who really looked after me, and I always thought of her as my second mother. To start with, the family was happy to have a baby in the house but then I didn't stop crying and crying. The only thing that would stop me was putting a tape recorder next to me playing *Zorba the Greek*, but that drove my siblings almost as mad as my crying.

We lived in a dusty neglected desert sort of town called Manbij in northern Syria, not far from the border with Turkey and about 20 miles west of the Euphrates river and the Tishrin dam which gave us electricity. My earliest memory is the long swish of my mother's dress – a light-coloured kaftan which fell to her ankles. She had long hair too, and we called her Ayee and my father Yaba and these are not Arabic words. The first fact to know about me is I'm a Kurd.

We were one of five Kurdish families on a street in a town that was mostly Arab; they were Bedouin but they looked down on us and called our area the Hill of the Foreigners. We had to speak their language at school and in the shops and could speak our Kurdish language Kurmanji only when we were at home. This was very hard for my parents, who didn't speak Arabic and were anyway illiterate. Also for my eldest brother Shiar, who other children made fun of at school because he couldn't speak Arabic.

Manbij is a folkish kind of place and strict about Islam, so my brothers had to go to the mosque, and if Ayee wanted to shop in the bazaar, one of them or my father had to accompany her. We are Muslims too but not so rigid. In the high school my sisters and cousins were the only girls who didn't cover their heads.

Our family had moved from our lands in a Kurdish village south of the city of Kobane because of a vendetta with a neighbouring village. We Kurds are tribal people and my family are from the big Kori Beg tribe, descended from a famous Kurdish resistance leader Kori Beg, which seems to mean almost every Kurd is a cousin. The next village were also Kori Beg but a different clan. The problem with them happened long before I was born, but we all knew the story. Both villages had sheep and one day some shepherd boys from the other village brought their flock to graze on our grass, so there was a fight with our shepherd boys. Shortly after that some of our relatives were going to the other village for a funeral and on the way were fired upon by two men from the other village. When our clan fired back one of their men was killed. They vowed revenge, so we all had to flee. That's how we ended up in Manbij.

People don't know much about Kurds – sometimes it seems to me we are completely unknown in the rest of the world. We are a proud people with our own language, food and culture and a long history going back 2,000 years when we were first recorded as Kurti. We are maybe 30 million people, but we have never had our own country. In fact we are the world's biggest stateless tribe. We hoped we would get our own homeland when the British and French divided up the defeated Ottoman Empire after the First World War, just as the Arabs thought they would get their own independence as promised after the Arab Revolt. The Allied powers even signed an agreement called the Treaty of Sèvres in 1920 which recognized an autonomous Kurdistan.

But the new Turkish leader Kemal Atatürk who had led his country to independence, would not accept it, and then oil was found in Mosul in what would have been Kurdistan and the treaty was never ratified. Actually two British and French diplomats called Mark Sykes and Georges Picot had already signed a secret pact to split the Levant between them and drawn their infamous line in the sand, from Kirkuk in Iraq to Haifa in Israel, to create the modern states of Iraq, Syria and Lebanon. So the Arabs were left under colonial rule, between borders which paid little heed to tribal and ethnic realities, and we Kurds were left divided between four countries, none of which likes us.

Today about half the Kurds live in Turkey, some in Iraq, some in Iran and about 2 million of us in Syria where we are the biggest minority, about 15 per cent. Even though our dialects are different I can always tell a Kurd from any other person in the world – first by the tongue, then by the look. Some of us live in cities like Istanbul, Tehran and Aleppo, but most live in the mountains and plateaus where Turkey, Syria, Iraq and Iran meet.

We are surrounded by enemies, so we have to remain strong. Our great Kurdish Shakespeare Ahmad-i Khani wrote in the seventeenth century that we are like 'towers on four corners surrounding the Turks and Persians ... both sides have made the Kurdish people targets for the arrows of their fate'. Yaba believes that one day there will be a Kurdistan, maybe in my lifetime. 'He who has a history has a future,' he always says.

The funny thing is many of the famous 'Arab' heroes are Kurds and no one admits it. Like Saladin, who fought off the Crusaders and kicked the Europeans out of Jerusalem, or Yusuf al-Azma, who led the Syrian forces fighting the French occupation in 1920 and died in battle. There is a huge painting of Saladin and his Arab armies in the reception hall of Assad's palace and we have so many squares and statues named after Yusuf al-Azma, but no one says they are Kurds.

Instead the Syrian regime call us *ajanib* or foreigners, even though we have lived here since before the Crusades. Many Kurds in Syria don't have ID cards, and without those orange cards you can't buy property, get government jobs, vote in elections or send your kids to high school.

I guess Turkey is the hardest place to be a Kurd. Atatürk launched a campaign called Turkification, and Turkey doesn't even recognize Kurds as a people but calls them mountain Turks. Our family live both sides of the border, and one of my aunts who lived in Turkey told us she couldn't even give her son a Kurdish name but had to call him Orhan, which is Turkish. Nasrine went to stay with her once and told us they don't speak Kurdish and turned off the radio when she played Kurdish music.

Here is another fact about Kurds. We have our own alphabet which Turkey does not recognize, and until not long ago you could be arrested there if you used the letters Q, W and X, which don't exist in the Turkish language. Imagine going to jail for a consonant!

We have a saying, 'Kurds have no friends but in the mountains.' We love mountains and we believe we are descended from children hidden in the mountains to escape Zuhak, an evil giant with two serpents growing from his shoulders, each of which had to be fed the brains of a boy every day. Finally, a clever blacksmith called Kawa, fed up with losing his sons, started feeding the serpents with sheep brains instead and hiding the boys until he had a whole army of them to slay the giant.

Kurds together always tell stories. Our most famous story is a Kurdish *Romeo and Juliet* called *Mem and Zin*. It's about an island ruled by a prince with two beautiful sisters he keeps locked up, one of whom he calls Zin. One day Zin and her sister escape to go to a festival disguised as men and meet two handsome musketeers, one of whom is Mem. The two pairs of sisters and musketeers fall in love and a lot of things happen, but basically Mem is imprisoned, then killed, and Zin dies of grief at her lover's grave. Even after death they are kept apart when a thorn bush springs up between them. The story starts by saying, 'If only there were harmony among us, if we were to obey a single one of us, he would reduce to vassalage Turks, Arabs and Persians, all of them,' and many Kurds say it symbolizes our struggle for a homeland. Mem represents the Kurdish people and Zin the Kurdish country, separated by unfortunate circumstances. Some people believe it's true and there is even a grave you can visit.

I grew up hearing this story but I don't really like it. It's quite long and I don't think it's realistic at all. Actually I preferred *Beauty and the Beast*, because that's based on something good, loving someone from the inside, for their personality, not the outside.

Before he got old and tired and stopped working and spent all his time smoking and grumbling about his sons not going to mosque, my father Yaba was a sheep and goat trader. He had about 60 acres of land, where he kept sheep and goats like his father before him going right back to my seventh grandfather, who had camels and sheep.

My elder siblings tell me that when he started he would buy just one goat a week in the market on Saturday then sell it elsewhere the following week for a small profit, but over time he had a flock of about 200. I guess selling sheep didn't make much money, as our house was just two rooms and a courtyard with a small kitchen which was a squash for so many people. But my eldest brother Shiar sent money, so we built another room where Ayee kept her sewing machine, which I played with when no one was looking. I slept there with her unless we had guests.

Shiar lives in Germany and is a film director who made a movie called *Walking* about a crazy old man who walks a lot in a Kurdish village in southern Turkey. The man makes friends with a poor boy who sells chewing gum, then their area gets taken over by the military. The film caused an outcry in Turkey because the old Kurdish man slaps a Turkish army officer, which some people protested shouldn't be shown – as if they can't tell the difference between a movie and real life.

I had never met Shiar as he left Syria in 1990 when he was seventeen, long before I was born, to avoid being conscripted and sent to fight in the Gulf War in Iraq – we were friends with the Americans in those days. Syria didn't want us Kurds to go to its universities or have government jobs but it did want us to fight in their army and join its Ba'ath party. Every schoolchild was supposed to join, but Shiar refused and managed to escape when he and another boy were marched to the party office to be signed up. He had always dreamt of being a movie director, which is strange because when he was growing up our house in Manbij didn't even have a TV, only a radio, as the religious people didn't approve. When he was twelve he made his own radio series with some classmates, and he sneaked every opportunity to watch other people's TVs. Somehow our family raised $4,500 for him to buy a fake Iraqi passport in Damascus, then he flew to Moscow to study. He didn't stay long in Russia but went to Holland, where he got asylum. There are not many Kurdish film-makers, so he is famous in our community, but we weren't supposed to mention him as the regime don't like his films.

Our family tree only shows men, but it didn't show Shiar in case anyone connected him with us and caused problems. I didn't understand why it shouldn't have women. Ayee was illiterate – she had got married to my dad when she was thirteen, which means that by my age today she had already been married four years and had a son. But she made all our clothes and she can tell you where any country in the world is on a map and always remember her way back from anywhere. Also she is good at adding things up, so she knew if the merchants in the bazaar were cheating her. All our family is good at maths except me. My grandfather on my mother's side had been arrested by the French for having a gun and shared a cell with a learned man who taught him to read, so because of that Ayee wanted us to be educated. My eldest sister Jamila had left school at twelve as girls in our tribe are not supposed to be educated and stayed at home and kept house. But after her, my other sisters – Nahda, Nahra and Nasrine – all went to school, just like the boys, Shiar, Farhad, Mustafa and Bland. We have a Kurdish saying: 'Male or female, the lion remains a lion.' Yaba said they could stay for as long as they passed the exams.

Each morning, I sat on the doorstep to watch them go, swinging their schoolbags and chatting with friends. The step was my favourite place to sit, playing with mud and watching people coming and going. Most of all I was waiting for someone in particular – the salep-man. If you haven't tried it, salep is a kind of smoothie from milk thickened with powdered roots of mountain orchids and flavoured with rose-water or cinnamon, ladled into a cup from a small aluminium cart, and it is delicious. I always knew when the salep-man was coming as the boom-box on his cart broadcast verses from the Koran, not music like other street vendors.

It was lonely when they had all gone, just Yaba smoking and clacking his worry beads if he didn't go to his sheep. To the right-hand side of the house, between us and our neighbours who were my uncle and cousins, was a tall cypress tree which was dark and scary. And on our roof were always stray cats and street dogs which made me shiver because if they came after me I couldn't run away. I don't like dogs, cats or anything that moves fast. There was a family of white cats with orange patches which spat and swore at anyone who came near and I hated them.

The only time I liked our roof was on hot summer nights when we slept up there, the darkness thick around us like a glove and a fresh breeze cooled by the emptiness of the desert. I loved lying on my back and staring up at the stars, so many and so far stretching into the beyond like a glittering walkway. That's when I first dreamt about being an astronaut, because in space you can float so your legs don't matter.

The funny thing is you can't cry in space. Because of zero gravity, if you cry the way you do on earth the tears won't fall but will gather in your eyes and form a liquid ball and spread into the rest of your face like a strange growth, so be careful.

2

The Walls of Aleppo

Aleppo, Syria, 2003–2008

People have always looked at me differently. My sisters are so pretty, particularly Nasrine with her long glossy mahogany hair and fair skin that freckles a little in sunshine. But me – well, I look more Arab, my front teeth are big and goofy, my eyes roll around and go cross-eyed and my glasses are always falling off my nose. And that's not all.

Maybe because Ayee was a bit old when she had me, forty-four, I was born too soon – forty days which is the amount of time Christians say their prophet Jesus fasted in the wilderness before his crucifixion. My brain didn't get enough oxygen and something happened that means the balance part doesn't work and it doesn't send proper signals to my legs, so they have a life of their own. They kick up when I am speaking, my ankles turn inwards, my toes point downwards, my heels point up and I can't walk. It's like I am forever stuck on tiptoes. Also my palms and fingers go convex instead of concave if I don't concentrate. Basically my extremities are like those Chinese fortune fishes that curl up and then are impossible to straighten.

When I didn't walk like other children, my parents took me to a doctor who said there was a missing connection in my brain that would form by the time I was five and then I would be able to walk, as long as they gave me plenty of protein and calcium. My mum made me eat lots of eggs and have vitamin injections, but my legs still didn't work. We went to lots of doctors. My brother Shiar called from Germany and gave them the name of a specialist to take me to in Aleppo. He laid me in a machine that was like a plastic coffin for an MRI scan. Afterwards he said I had something called balance deficiency which is a kind of cerebral palsy. I didn't understand these long words but I could see it was scary for Ayee and Yaba. The doctor said I would need surgery and physical therapy.

Also as Manbij was a dusty neglected place, and maybe because of the gangs of cats and dogs, I got asthma so badly that I often wheezed until I was blue in the face. So when I was four we moved to Aleppo where I could get medical help and where my sister Nahda and brother Bland could go to university. Nahda was so smart she came top of all the students in Manbij and was the first girl in our family to go to university. She was studying law and I thought maybe she would be a famous lawyer.

The Walls of Aleppo

Aleppo is a very historic place – some say it is the oldest inhabited city in the world – and the biggest city in Syria. You could get everything there. We lived in a Kurdish neighbourhood in the north-west called Sheikh Maqsoud, which was high up and looked over the whole city with its pale stone buildings that shone almond-pink in the late-afternoon sun. In the middle was the walled fortress on a mound which had watched over Aleppo for perhaps a thousand years.

Our new home was a fifth-floor apartment at 19 George al-Aswad Street, named after a Christian who used to own the land – around 10 per cent of our population was Christian and the Christian cemetery was just near by. I liked it better than Manbij because there were no cats and dogs scratching and howling on the roof or scary dark tree from which I had to hide under the blanket, and it was bigger with four rooms, a bathroom and two balconies from which you could watch the world go by. My mum was happier having lots of Kurds around. And best of all, one of the rooms was a living room where we watched TV.

My brothers Shiar and Farhad were both living abroad and Mustafa stayed in Manbij running a company digging water wells, which was good business because we lived in times of drought. At the beginning all my sisters were with us in Aleppo, but Jamila, Nahda and Nahra got married one after another (I cried each time!). After Jamila's wedding when people came to our house in Aleppo to congratulate the bride and groom, I sat on the sofa glaring at our cousin Mohammed who she was marrying. Jamila might have had a temper that came and went like a gust of wind, particularly if anyone tried to interfere with her housekeeping, but she had looked after all of us.

After that it was just me, Bland and Nasrine. Bland slept in the TV room along with me, Ayee and Mustafa when he was not away travelling. Nasrine had a tiny room of her own.

Our block had six floors, but the one above ours was condemned so we were the highest. All the other people in the building were Kurdish but came from different towns. The neighbours on our floor had children – four girls, Parwen, Nermin, Hemrin and Tallin, and one boy, Kawa, who was the youngest. I loved them, but whenever we played games I always felt like the weakest link and often they ran away from me, laughing as I tried to drag myself after them in my odd way like a rabbit. I looked like a rabbit with my teeth and I crawl-jumped like a rabbit. Another family two floors down had a pet tortoise which they would bring upstairs. I loved to have it on my lap and would sit and watch when they ran away. I was neither comfortable nor welcomed in the kids' world.

My substitute for all that fun deficiency was TV. I watched everything, starting with cartoons and Disney DVDs. My family loved football, so we all watched that together. Then when I was eight and we got a satellite dish, I watched documentaries about history and science. And much later when we got a computer I discovered Google and began collecting every bit of information I could get. Thank you, Sergey Brin, I would like to meet you one day.

To start with I went to a physical-therapy centre called the Fraternity. It looked like a traditional Syrian house with a big courtyard with swings and a fountain. There was no lift so I had to use the guardrail to pull myself up the stairs. The therapists there smiled but then made me do complicated things like balance training using rubber balls. They also strapped me into a device with bands fixed round my waist and down to my legs to try and get me to stand straight. It looked like something that might have been in one of Assad's torture chambers.

I was supposed to go to the Fraternity to exercise twice a week, but I kept having asthma attacks and ended up in hospital so many times that the doctors there got to know me. The attacks always seemed to be in the middle of the night and sometimes the air became so squeezed from my wheezing lungs that Ayee thought I was going to die. Gentle Jamila always comforted me. After she left home to marry, Bland and Nasrine came with me instead. Anything seemed to set me off. Worst of all was smoking – just about all men in Syria smoke and some women. No one was supposed to smoke in our apartment, but I could smell it even from the ground floor. I always seemed to have attacks at holiday times – I spent four Eid festivals in hospital.

In my country there are almost no facilities for disabled people, and the asthma attacks happened so often that I couldn't go to school. My third sister Nahra had not got good enough grades to go to university, so until she got married she was at home too. She was much more interested in beauty and make-up than my other sisters and we always had to wait while she dressed up, but she didn't think my disability should be an excuse not to learn. Not only did she teach me the rules of football, but when I was six she taught me to read and write in Arabic, making me write the same sentence over and over again until it filled a sheet and I was driven crazy.

I learnt quickly. Nasrine went to the local school to beg textbooks for me and I would finish them in a couple of weeks. Once I could read, my world was books, TV and sitting on the balcony. From there, among the plants, I could look across to other roofs with their flapping laundry, satellite dishes and water tanks. Beyond them were pencil-thin minarets from where came the prayer call five times a day and which in the evenings were bathed in magical green light. Mostly I kept an eye on our street. Both sides were lined with apartment blocks like ours – the only shops were a grocery and a store selling football jerseys. The road wasn't too busy, every so often a honking car or a motorbike, and every morning a man would come pushing his cart selling gas cylinders for heating and cooking. I guess he was a Christian as his music box always played Christmas carols.

On his cart like everywhere there were pictures of our dictator Bashar al-Assad. Our leaders in this part of the world like their personality cults. Everything was named Assad. Assad, Assad, Assad – Assad Lake, the Assad Academy, even the Assad Writing Club. Billboards appeared on the street with different pictures of him almost every week, some as the serious statesman meeting other heads of state, others meant to show him as a fatherly figure, smiling and waving or cycling with one of his children seated on the back and with feel-good slogans like '*Kullna ma'ak*' – 'We are all with you'. People said the eyes had been tinted to look bluer. I feel I was deceived by all these things.

There were also pictures of his late father Hafez, who started the whole family ruling enterprise back in 1970. Hafez had been born poor, one of eleven children, but had risen to be head of the air force about the time my dad did national service, and then ran the country for decades after seizing power in a coup. Like us, the Assads were minorities – they came from the Alawite clan – but they were Shias, while most Syrians are Sunni like us. Maybe that made them insecure, for they ran our country as a police state with fifteen different intelligence agencies, and if people protested they were locked up or killed. Hafez survived several assassination attempts, but in the end he died naturally of a heart attack in 2000, the year after I was born.

The plan had been for him to be succeeded by his daredevil eldest son Basil, who was an army officer and horse-riding champion. But Basil loved flashy fast cars and died in 1994 when he crashed his Mercedes at high speed on the road to Damascus airport. So the shy, thin second son Bashar took over, the one people called Mama's boy. To start with people were happy about that. Unlike his father, who was trained as a pilot in the Soviet Union, Bashar had studied in England as an eye doctor – he was doing postgraduate ophthalmology at the Western Eye Hospital in London – and his wife Asma was British born (her father works as a cardiologist in London). We were proud of having a young handsome President with a beautiful wife who travelled the world, even meeting the Queen, and thought they'd be more open-minded and change things. And at the beginning they did – he released hundreds of political prisoners, allowed intellectuals to have political meetings and authorized the launch of the first independent newspaper for decades. He reduced the retirement age in the army to get rid of his father's old guard. People called it the Damascus Spring.

Unfortunately, within two years, everything went back to how it had been. Maybe because of that old guard who didn't like changes. Once again people lived in fear of the Mukhabarat, our secret police, and never quite said what they thought as they didn't know who was listening or watching.

* * *

The Walls of Aleppo

My favourite saying is 'Laugh as long as you breathe, love as long as you live,' and I don't see why anyone would want to wallow in misery when there is such a beautiful world out there. It's one of my Nujeen principles. Another one is I don't believe anyone is born evil, even Assad. The problem is he grew up as this spoilt boy who would inherit his father's kingdom. It was like the Assad family owned us and believed they should never give it up. We never talked about Assad, even at home between ourselves. We knew they have agents everywhere. The walls have ears, we used to say, so don't talk.

I watched things too and would know when men had come home from work in the late afternoon as the sweet smell of tobacco would rise up from them lighting up their hookah pipes and start to tickle my treacherous lungs. Sometimes as I watched the shadows move across the street and caught sight of figures disappearing down winding alleys I wished I could wander. What would it be like to lose yourself in a warren of narrow streets?

Aleppo was a place where many tourists came and which everyone says is beautiful with its medieval citadel, Great Mosque and the world's oldest covered souk selling goods from along the Silk Road like Indian spices, Chinese silks and Persian carpets. Our apartment was high so if one of my family helped me stand I could see the citadel lit up at night on a hill in the middle. How I wished I could go and see it. I begged my mum to take me but she couldn't because of all the steps.

All I saw was our room and the parts of my home I could drag myself to with my rabbit-jumping. My family did try to take me out but it was so much effort as we had no lift, so I had to be carried all the way down five flights, and then the streets were so full of potholes that it was difficult even for an able-bodied person to walk. The only place I could go was my uncle's house because it was near by and his building had a lift, so I became less interested in going out. When I did, after five minutes I would want to be back, so I guess you could say I was the one who locked herself up.

Sometimes I saw Yaba looking at me sadly. He never told me off even when I flooded the bathroom by playing water-polo and he would fetch me anything I liked – or send my brothers – whether it was fried chicken from a restaurant in the middle of the night or the chocolate and coconut cake I loved. I tried to look happy for him. He never let me do anything for myself. Nasrine used to get cross. If I was thirsty and demanded a drink, my father would insist she fetched it even if the bottle was just across the table from me. Once I saw her crying. 'Yaba,' she said, 'now we're all here, but what will Nuj do when we all die?'

The worst thing about being disabled is you can't go away and cry somewhere on your own. You have no privacy. Sometimes you just have a bad mood and you want to cry and push out all that negative energy, but I couldn't because I couldn't go anywhere. I always had to rely on people. I tried to avoid people looking at the way I walked. When I met someone for the first time my mum would recount the whole story of my birth then go on about how smart I am, as if to say 'Look, she can't walk but she is not mentally disabled.' I would just stay silent and stare at the TV.

The TV became my school and my friend, and I spent all my time with adults, like my uncles who lived near by. I never played with toys. When relatives came to visit, they sometimes brought dolls or soft toys, but these just stayed on a shelf. Mustafa says I was born with the mind of an adult. When I tried to make friends my own age it didn't work. My eldest brother Shiar has a daughter Rawan who is a year and a half younger than me and she and her mum came to stay with us several times. I really wanted to be her friend so I would do anything with her, play even the most boring game or let her use me as her model for experiments in hairdressing. But as soon as anyone came who could walk I would be brushed off. One day when she was five and I was seven, I asked her why she didn't play with me. 'Because you can't walk,' she replied. Sometimes I felt I was just an extra member of the world's population.

3

The Girl on TV

Apart from facts I like dates. For example, 19 April 1770 was the day Captain James Cook found Australia and 4 September 1998 was the date Google was established. My least favourite date is 16 March. That is a black day in the history of Kurds when in 1988, in the final days of the Iran–Iraq War, around twenty of Saddam Hussein's fighter jets swooped down and dropped a deadly mixture of mustard gas and nerve agents on Kurds in the city of Halabja in northern Iraq. The town had fallen to the Iranians who had joined forces with local Kurds, and Saddam wanted to punish them. We call that day Bloody Friday. Thousands of men, women and children were killed – even today we don't know how many, but perhaps 5,000 – and thousands more were left with their skin all melted and with difficulties breathing. Afterwards lots of babies were born with deformities.

Every year on that day our Kurdish TV channel would play mournful songs about Halabja and show old film, which made me so sad. It was awful to see the clouds of white, black and yellow smoke rising up in tall columns over the town after the bombing, then people running and wailing, dragging their children behind them or on their shoulders, and bodies piling up. I watched one film where people said the gas smelled of sweet apples and after that I couldn't eat an apple. I hate that day – I wish I could delete it from the calendar. Saddam was an even worse dictator than Assad. Yet the West kept supporting Saddam for years, even giving him weapons. Sometimes it seems that nobody likes the Kurds. Our list of sorrows is endless.

March is actually the best time and the worst time for Kurds because it is the month of our annual festival Newroz, marking the start of spring, a festival that we share with the Persians. For us it also commemorates the day when the evil child-eating tyrant Zuhak was defeated by the blacksmith Kawa.

In the days running up to Newroz the flat would be filled with heavenly smells of cooking, Ayee and my sisters making dolma, vine leaves rolled around a stuffing of tomato, eggplant, zucchini and onion, and potatoes filled with spicy mince (apart from one potato that we always leave empty for luck for whoever gets it). And it was the one time of year when I went out. A few days before Newroz we and all our neighbours would festoon our balconies with coloured lights in red, green, white and yellow, the colours of the national flag of Kurdistan. On the actual day we would dress up in national dress and set off in a mini-bus.

Of course the regime didn't like it and put lots of police on the streets that day. They only allowed the festival because they knew how stubborn we Kurds are and feared there would be riots if they banned it. But you still needed an official permit which was hard to get, and we weren't allowed to enjoy our festivities on the local streets. Instead we had to go to a sort of wasteland called Haql al-rmy on the outskirts of Aleppo, which the army used for rifle practice and which literally means shooting field in English. It was a bleak rocky place, so we took lots of rugs to sit on and to spread our picnics on.

To be honest, sometimes I hoped it would be banned because I hated going to it. First it was almost like torture to get me down those five floors of stairs. Then when we got there it was totally loud and crowded, and so uncomfortable sitting on the hard ground. I couldn't even see the folk dancing or the march with our national songs. And we had to be careful what we said because among the revellers were vendors selling balloons and ice-cream and candyfloss and people thought they were spies for Assad's intelligence. Actually we were always careful. In the evening there would be a bonfire which people would dance around and fireworks would light up the sky.

Then a week or so later would come the arrests of the organizers, the people who had set up the stage for the musicians and sound systems. In 2008, police shot dead three young men celebrating Newroz in a Kurdish town and there were calls for it to be banned. Rather than having an outright clash with all the Kurds, the regime announced that from then on that date would be Mother's Day, and any festivities would be to celebrate that. See how wily these Assads are.

That was the year I missed Newroz because the doctors decided to try and lengthen my Achilles tendons to enable me to stretch out my feet and put my ankles on the ground, instead of always standing on tiptoe. I woke in Al Salam hospital with the bottom halves of my legs encased in plaster. It felt as if my feet were on fire, and I cried. I missed my eldest sister, gentle Jamila, who had got married the previous year and moved away. Bland had finished his studies and got a job as an accountant for a trading company and Nasrine had just started at Aleppo University to study physics in the footsteps of my sister Nahda. I was happy for them but it meant I was alone at home all day with Ayee and Yaba.

One day I was sitting on the rug on the big balcony when Ayee came with my uncle Ali, who had just been visiting relatives in the city of Homs. 'Your uncle has something for you,' she said. Uncle Ali handed me a tissue box and laughed as my face fell. A box of tissues didn't seem much of a gift.

'Look inside,' he said. I did and there among the tissues was a small tortoise. Homs was famous for its tortoises. I was so happy I sat with the box on my lap all day long. I loved tracing the patterns on her domed shell with my finger and watching her little head poke out, all grey and wrinkled like snakeskin with little beady black eyes. That first day she barely moved and I was terrified I had damaged her as I was notorious in my family for breaking everything I touched. For the first few days I would check her every two minutes to make sure she was still alive. We kept her on the balcony, fed her salad leaves and called her Sriaa, which is Arabic for fast because she was very slow. Even slower than me.

The only person who didn't like the tortoise was Yaba. He complained she was *haram* or unIslamic. I laughed, but then summer came and we slept outside on the balcony and one night we were all awoken by loud cursing. The tortoise had climbed on to my father and he was furious.

The next day I couldn't see Sriaa anywhere. I looked all over the balcony, becoming more and more suspicious. Finally, I went to Yaba. 'Where is she?' I demanded. 'I've taken her to be sold,' he said. 'It's for the best, Nujeen, it's cruel to keep animals confined.'

'No!' I screamed. 'The tortoise was mine and was happy here. How do you know what will happen to her now?' I bawled my eyes out.

I couldn't complain of course as he had got rid of her for religious reasons. And afterwards I was secretly relieved. I had been so worried about Sriaa dying. If you hold a tortoise by its tail it will die. I wouldn't have been able to cope with that.

With the other children from the building off at school, and no more tortoise to watch, there was nothing to do but watch TV. The satellite dish meant my room suddenly opened into a whole new world. National Geographic, the History Channel, Arts & Entertainment … I liked history programmes and wildlife programmes – my favourite animal is the lion, king of the jungle – and scariest is the piranha which can eat a human in ninety seconds.

Mostly I watched documentaries. Everything I know about aliens or space or astronauts like Neil Armstrong and Yuri Gagarin is from documentaries. I was very cross with Gagarin because he said that when he became the first man to cross the Karman line into outer space in 1961 he didn't see any signs of God. That is very hard for us Muslims. But later I saw another programme which said he didn't actually say that. We are always being deceived.

The TV was on all the time, its blue aquarium light flickering night and day until sometimes Ayee or Mustafa shouted at me to turn it off so they could sleep. As I didn't go to school, sometimes I watched till 3 a.m. then got up at 8.30 a.m. to start again. My favourite day was Tuesday when they broadcast an Arabic version of *Who Wants to be a Millionaire?*

The Girl on TV

I loved quiz shows. There was also one every evening at six called *Al Darb* which means The Track where people competed as teams. I could usually answer all the questions.

It wasn't a big TV – 20 inches – and it had a big crack on one side because once I grabbed the TV table to try and stand up and the TV fell on me. I cried, not because I was hurt, but because I thought the TV would never work again. Every so often Bland got cross with me. 'Nujeen, you've convinced yourself that you love home and TV and that it's better than going out, but no one really wants to be indoors all the time,' he said. I ignored him. But sometimes I did wonder what other disabled people did. Then I went back to the TV.

Ayee, Nasrine and I liked watching tennis. The US Open, the French Open, the Australian Open and best of all Wimbledon with the umpires so smartly uniformed in green and purple and the grass courts so perfect like carpets. Soon I knew all the rules. Ayee liked Andy Murray, while I liked Roger Federer and Nasrine liked Nadal, just as in football I liked Barcelona and Nasrine liked Real Madrid.

The one time everyone watched together was during the World Cup in 2010. My family loves football! As usual everyone in the area hung flags for their favourite team. I hung an Argentina flag from the balcony for Lionel Messi. Our neighbour had an Italian flag. But I was distracted and kept crying for my second mother Jamila. The doctors had said I would get better as I was older but my feet, which were supposed to have straightened, seemed more curled up than ever.

Eventually my brother Farhad in England found out about a famous orthopaedic surgeon in Aleppo. He was so sought after that it took months to get an appointment, so we went early one morning to his surgery to get a ticket and found villagers who had been waiting all night. We were number 51. Every patient got five minutes and we finally saw him in the late afternoon.

When he saw my feet he was cross and told my parents they shouldn't have let them deteriorate, that I should have been doing exercises. He said I would need to have three operations together as soon as possible and sent us to the hospital for blood tests, then he would operate the following day. He did a new operation on my ankles and two others to lengthen my knee ligaments, which had become too short from lack of exercise. It cost my family $4,000, paid for by my second eldest brother Mustafa from his water wells, and this time the whole of my legs were in plaster, from hip to ankle, only my toes poking out, and I had to lie flat.

I was supposed to stay in hospital but insisted on coming out after one night to watch the football. I was desperate for Argentina to win, otherwise Spain. However, the pain was so bad I screamed all the way back in the taxi and again at home, until I drove Mustafa and Bland out of the room because they couldn't bear it.

Finally, the pain stopped but I was in plaster for forty days, which felt like a very long time. Then Mustafa paid for a special brace to put my legs in to strengthen the muscles.

They looked like robot legs, and oh they were agony! I had to wear them ten hours a day and I complained so much. But after a week I got used to them and they meant that for the first time I could stand with the help of a walker. I could see parts of the apartment I never normally went into like the kitchen and I could see the citadel from the balcony without any help. Ayee says it was like I was newborn.

About that time I started watching an American soap opera. It was called *Days of Our Lives*, about two rival families called the Hortons and the Bradys living in a fictional town in Illinois and a mafia family called the DiMeras and their love-triangles and feuds. They all had beautiful big houses with lots of clothes and appliances and each child had their own bedroom. One of the men was a doctor in an immaculate shiny hospital, not at all like Al Salam where I had been. Their lives were so different to ours. To start with I didn't understand what was going on and sometimes the story was odd, with characters coming back from the dead, but after a while I caught up. I watched it with Ayee and it drove Nasrine mad. 'What on earth do you see in this?' she asked.

We had our own family soap opera. My parents were desperate about Mustafa not getting married. As second son, he should have got married after Shiar in 1999, but first he said he should wait for Jamila, then once she was married he said he needed to devote himself to work as he was our main provider. But now he was thirty-five which in our culture is very old to be unmarried. We have arranged marriages – not love-matches, which from what I could see from *Days of Our Lives* was not a very good system. My mother kept going to meet suitable brides from our tribe, but Mustafa always refused to take it further and just laughed. It didn't matter whether he was there in the apartment or not – it seemed like all anyone talked about. I hated it. Whenever they raised the subject, I shouted, 'Not again!' and covered my ears.

4

Days of Rage

Aleppo, 2011

It was 25 January 2011, just after my twelfth birthday, and I was watching *Days of Our Lives*, worrying that I might be a psychopath because my favourite characters always seemed to be the bad guys, when Bland rushed in from work and grabbed the remote. I looked at him in astonishment. Everyone knew I was in charge of the TV.

Bland is usually so calm and laid back that I always feel there is a part of him nobody knows, but this time he seemed to be spinning like one of those dust-devils we used to get in the desert. Now, not only had he taken the remote but he switched over to Al Jazeera. My family all know I don't like the news: it was always bad – Afghanistan, Iraq, Lebanon, war after war in fellow Muslim countries pretty much since I was born.

'Something has happened!' he said. On the screen we could see thousands of people gathering in the main square in Cairo, waving flags and demanding the removal of their long-time President Hosni Mubarak. I was scared. Dictators fire on people. We knew that. I did not want to see it. I started shaking my head.

'I was watching my programme,' I protested. One of what I call my 'disability benefits' is that my brothers and sisters all knew they weren't supposed to upset me. Even when I threw Nasrine's things out of the window, like her blue pen and the CD of Kurdish songs she used to play all the time.

As I predicted, soon came the teargas and rubber bullets and water cannons to drive the demonstrators away. The thud of the bullets made me jump. After that Bland let me switch back. But the protests didn't stop. Mustafa, Bland and Nasrine talked of nothing else, and whenever I was out of the room they switched to the news. I gave up trying to resist and soon I too was glued to Al Jazeera watching those crowds in Tahrir Square grow and grow. Many of the protesters were young people like Bland and Nasrine and had painted the Egyptian flag on their faces or sported bandannas on their heads in red, white and black.

One day, we watched – hearts in mouth – as a column of tanks advanced into the square like monsters. Dozens of protesters bravely blocked their way and I could hardly watch. Then something astonishing happened. The tanks didn't open fire but stopped. The crowd chanted and people climbed on top, scrawling 'Mubarak Must Go!' on their sides, and we could see they were even chatting to the soldiers.

A couple of days later, me, Bland and Nasrine were again on the edge of the sofa as crowds of pro-Mubarak supporters pushed their way into the square like a demon cavalry on horses and camels. They were beaten back by the protesters, who hurled stones and ripped out paving slabs from the square to use as shields. The tanks formed a line between the two groups and it was hard to see what was going on, as there was so much dust and things were on fire. Finally, the Mubarakites were chased out and the democracy people erected barricades of street signs and bits of metal fencing and burnt-out cars to stop them coming back.

Where would it end? we wondered. The protesters made a kind of tent city in the square with a field hospital to treat their wounded, with sections of the crowd handing out food and water and even doing haircuts and shaves. It almost looked like a festival, a bit like our annual Newroz. I could see children my age stamping on pictures of Mubarak. The journalists reporting it all were excited too. They even had a name for it. The Arab Spring, they called it. For us that sounded a bit like our Damascus Spring and that hadn't ended well at all.

The occupation went on for eighteen days. Then around 6 p.m. on 11 February, Nahda and Nasrine had just come back from my uncle's wedding which woke me up from a nap. We switched on the TV and there was Egypt's Vice President announcing, 'President Hosni Mubarak has decided to step down.' Soon came the news that the Mubaraks had been flown out in an army helicopter to exile in the Red Sea resort of Sharm El-Sheikh. That was it, gone after three decades. I was happy for Egypt. Afterwards there were fireworks, soldiers climbing out of their tanks to hug the demonstrators, people singing and whistling. Was it that easy? If I fell asleep again in the afternoon would I wake up and find Gaddafi gone from Libya? Or even Assad?

And Egypt wasn't all. At the time we hadn't realized it was a 'thing', but the Arab Spring had actually begun the previous December in Tunisia, when a poor twenty-six-year-old fruit-seller named Mohamed Bouazizi poured kerosene over his body and set fire to himself outside a town hall. This was shocking for us Muslims as our holy Koran prohibits the use of fire on Allah's creation, so he must have been completely desperate. We didn't know if he would go to heaven or hell. His family said he had been fed up with local officials humiliating him and had become desperate when they confiscated his fruit cart which was their whole livelihood. When he died of his burns in January there were massive protests in the centre of Tunis and ten days later President Zine al-Abidine Ben Ali and his family ran away to Saudi Arabia after twenty-three years of power.

Soon every day on the TV there were uprisings somewhere new. Yemen, Bahrain, Jordan, Libya, Algeria, Morocco, even Oman, all had demonstrations against their rulers – it was like an epidemic across North Africa and the Middle East. Of course we knew about the forty years of Assads, but we hadn't realized how long all these dictators had been in power. People would gather after Friday prayers then swarm into the streets and congregate in some central square. Days of Rage they called it.

When would it be Syria? Like those other countries, our population was mostly young and unemployed, and we had had our rights trampled on by a dictator and the rich elite. Even in my room on the fifth floor I could sense that the whole country seemed to be holding its breath. Nasrine said that at the university nobody was talking about anything else. My brothers and sisters came home with reports of odd incidents – a Kurdish man in the north-eastern city al-Hasakah had set fire to himself; some small demonstrations here and there; even a protest in Damascus after police assaulted a merchant in one of the main souks. But nothing quite caught hold.

When the spark finally did come it was in an unlikely place – the small farming town of Deraa in the south-west, near the border with Jordan, which we knew as a bastion of support for the regime that had long sent its sons to top posts. In recent years, they had produced a prime minister, a foreign minister and a head of the ruling Ba'ath party.

The catalyst was the arrest in late February of a group of teenage boys who had been scrawling anti-regime graffiti on

school walls. *'Al-Shaab yureed eskat el nizam!'* they wrote –
'The people want to topple the regime' – just as the crowds
had shouted in Cairo. 'Bashar out!' wrote another. A third was
writing, 'Your turn next, doctor,' when he was spotted by
security forces.

Over the next few days they rounded up ten more teenagers, making fifteen in total, and took them to the local Political
Security Directorate – I told you we have many secret police
– which was under the control of General Atef Najeeb, the
President's cousin, who everyone was scared of.

Since Assad father's time, and the Six Day War in 1967
when Israel seized our Golan Heights from the Sea of Galilee
in the south to Mount Hermon in the north, our police and
security services have had absolute power to arrest and detain
anyone indefinitely without trial. They use the excuse that
we are in a permanent state of war with 'the Zionist entity',
which is what we call Israel, though when we fought them
again in the 1973 war we didn't get back the land. Assad's
jails are notorious for torture. People say death is easier than
a Syrian prison, though I don't know how anyone would
know that.

Soon there were reports that those boys were being beaten
and tortured, the usual Assad specialities like pulling out
fingernails and electric shocks to their private parts. Their
desperate parents went to the authorities and were told by
General Najeeb, 'Forget your children, go and make more.'
Can you imagine? Round the country young people tried to

organize a Day of Rage in support of the boys. I saw Nasrine and Bland looking at a Facebook page called 'The Syrian Revolution against Bashar al-Assad 2011', but they quickly closed it. We were scared even to look at the page.

Deraa is a very tribal area, and the arrested boys were from all the largest clans. And like many farmers we knew, its people were struggling because of a severe drought which had been going on for the last four years and they couldn't compete with cheap imports from Turkey and China. Instead of helping them, the government had cut subsidies. They were angry too at the way General Najeeb had been running the area as his personal fiefdom.

So, on 18 March, after Friday prayers, when the families of the missing marched on the house of the Deraa governor and started a sit-in to demand their release, they were accompanied by local religious and community leaders. Riot police used water cannon and teargas to try and disperse them, then armed police came and opened fire. Four people were killed. When people saw the blood they went crazy. Ambulances couldn't get through because of the security forces, so protesters had to carry their wounded to the ancient mosque in the Old City which they turned into a makeshift hospital.

Two days after that protesters set fire to the local Ba'ath party headquarters and other government buildings. President Assad sent an official delegation to offer condolences to the relatives of those killed, and sacked the governor and transferred General Najeeb.

It was too late. Now it was our turn. Our revolution had begun.

Predictably (dictators are so uninventive), Assad's first response was to send tanks into Deraa to crush the protests. Maybe because our army is mainly Alawite like the Assads, they didn't hold back as the Egyptian tanks had done. Instead they attacked the mosque, which had become a kind of head-quarters for protesters, and they did so with such force they left its ancient walls splattered with blood. The funerals of the people killed then turned into mass rallies. These in turn were fired on and more people killed, so there would be more funerals and even more people would turn out.

The government then issued a decree to cut taxes and raise state salaries, which only made everyone even angrier. At the next funeral the following day, tens of thousands of people gathered, shouting, 'We don't want your bread, we want dignity!' Then, at the end of March, Assad gave a speech in parliament denouncing the protesters as 'sectarian extremists' and 'foreign terrorists'. 'Such conspiracies don't work with our country or people,' he raged. 'We tell them you have only one choice which is to learn from your failure.'

We Syrians were shocked by that speech. 'He's treating us like traitors!' said Bland. Deraa was under siege, but weekly anti-government rallies began in other cities, the details shared on Facebook and YouTube. Throughout April and May there were protests in Homs, Hama, Damascus, Raqqa – spreading from Latakia on the Mediterranean coast to the rural northern regions bordering Turkey and the eastern province of Deir al-Zour where our oil comes from.

Each time they were met with a show of force as the government thought it could just crush the protests. Hundreds of people were being killed. But it didn't stop. Across the country people were shouting, 'With our souls, with our blood, we sacrifice to you, Deraa!'

Soon no one spoke of anything else. Even Mustafa's refusal to get married was forgotten. The air was electric, almost crackling. Revolution! It was like the history programmes I watched. We were full of excitement at the thought that we were going to get rid of the Assads. Suddenly people were talking about everything that had been unthinkable. It was beautiful. People made up songs against Assad. I made curses against Assad which I sometimes said out loud.

We Kurds thought we might finally get our Kurdistan, or Rojavo as we call it. Some banners on the streets read, 'Democracy for Syria. Federalism for Syrian Kurdistan'. But Yaba said we didn't understand. Older people like him knew the regime was dangerous because they had witnessed the 1980s in Hama when Hafez al-Assad and his brother Rifat quelled protests from the Muslim Brotherhood by massacring 10,000 people and pulverized the city. So they knew what the Assads would do.

The regime seemed deaf and blind to what people were demanding. Instead of real change Assad announced new things to try and appease different sectors of the population. He legalized the wearing of niqab by female schoolteachers which had been banned just the year before. To try and stop us Kurds joining the protests, Assad even passed a Presidential decree which gave citizenship to around 300,000 Kurds who had been stateless since the 1960s. For the first time ever, his spokesman came on state TV to wish Kurds a happy Newroz and played a Kurdish song.

It wasn't enough – what people wanted was less corruption and more freedom. Calls for reform became calls for the removal of Assad. Protesters ripped down the latest posters of Bashar – in jeans kneeling to plant a tree – and set fire to them and even tore down statues of his late father whose name we had barely dared whisper.

Most of this we watched on Al Jazeera or YouTube – Syrian TV didn't show it of course. Our best source of information was Mustafa, because he had started a business bringing trucks from Lebanon so was always driving across the country and seeing things. Like Yaba, he said our regime was tougher than the others. However, when he saw how that first protest in Deraa spread to Homs and Hama, he changed his mind.

He told us that in Hama there were so many people it was like a human wave had taken over the central square. Hama was the town where all those people had been massacred in 1982, and many of the protesters were orphans of that massacre. They poured into the streets after Friday prayers and as usual the regime retaliated. Three army trucks with large guns appeared and opened fire on them, killing seventy people. The men in the front row shouted the word 'Peacefully!' as they were felled. The killings incensed the town and soon the entire square was full.

'This is it,' Mustafa told us. 'By the third week it will be finished.'

Then he happened to be in the Kurdish town of Derik in south-east Turkey near the border when there was a birthday celebration for Abdulhamid Haji Darwish, head of Syria's Kurdish Democratic Progressive Party, at which everyone was discussing how we Kurds should respond to the revolution. All Kurds thought the regime finished and the discussion was how to make sure we got our own state or at least some autonomy like the Kurds in northern Iraq. They had sent someone to Baghdad to meet Jalal Talabani, the President of Iraq, and also a Kurd, to ask his opinion. He said the Assad regime wouldn't fall. That wasn't what people wanted to hear, so they said, 'Oh, Talabani has got old.'

It turned out he was right – he knew what was going on.

* * *

Syria wasn't the same as Egypt and Tunisia. Assad had learnt from his father the brutal way he had put down the Hama revolt, and even before that from our French masters. Back in 1925 when we were under French rule, Muslims, Druze and Christians together rose up in what we call the Great Revolt. The French responded with an artillery bombardment so massive that it flattened an entire quarter of the Old City of Damascus. That area is now known as al-Hariqa which means the Conflagration. They killed thousands of people and held public executions in the central Marja Square as a warning. After that the rebellion was crushed and we continued under French rule for another two decades until 1946.

Maybe because we didn't remember this history, we young people were sure there had to be change. When we heard that Assad was going to make another speech in June 2011 we expected he would finally announce some major reform. Instead he again took a hard line, denouncing what he called a conspiracy against Syria and blaming 'saboteurs' backed by foreign powers and 'religious extremists' who he claimed had taken advantage of the unrest. He said no reform was possible while the chaos continued. It was clear that he, or maybe his family, had no intention of giving up power. Like I said, they thought they owned us.

After that there started to be organized resistance. Hundreds of different rebel groups got together in what they called the Free Syrian Army or FSA and began to prepare for war. Most were young and inexperienced and untrained, but some were disgruntled members of Assad's own army. There were even reports that senior army officers had defected and joined the FSA. Kurds didn't join the FSA as we had our own militias, the YPG or People's Protection Units.

Assad simply stepped up the military action. Much of his firepower in those early days was trained on Homs, where my tortoise came from and which was one of the first places to rise up. Homs is our third largest city, and Sunnis, Shias, Alawites and Christians had lived side by side there, just as in Aleppo. The people didn't give up, particularly in the old neighbourhood of Babr al-Amr, even though Assad's forces were pulverizing the place. Soon it was known as the capital of the revolution. We thought that, when they saw all the killing, the Western powers would intervene as they had in Libya. There they had created a no-fly zone to stop Colonel Gaddafi from using his air force against protesters, and since April they had been launching airstrikes against regime targets like Gaddafi's compound in Tripoli and otherwise helping the rebels. By August the rebels had seized Tripoli and taken over. By October Gaddafi was dead, caught like a rat in a hole, and his body displayed in a freezer just like he had done to his opponents. But our opposition was divided, and it seemed the West did not know how to respond. Foreigners left the country and embassies started to close. By the end of 2011 much of the country was an open battle-ground between the resistance and military. Mustafa said it was causing chaos, which was good for his business as he didn't have to pay customs duties, but then the FSA started setting up checkpoints in their areas just as the regime did. Yaba was worried about him, so he didn't tell us that much.

The funny thing was for us it all seemed far off, not just for me on the fifth floor at 19 George al-Aswad Road, but even for Bland and my sisters. Even though we were the biggest city, Aleppo had not really joined the revolution. Maybe because we were the commercial and industrial centre of Syria and had lots of wealthy people, there were many loyal to the regime, worried about the effect of instability on their businesses. Also we had many minorities, Christians, Turkomans, Armenians, Assyrians, Jews, Circassians, Greeks and of course Kurds, and they were unsure about joining the opposition who were mostly Sunni Arabs and, people said, were getting help from Saudi Arabia and Qatar. It was kind of weird, like there were two parallel worlds. There was this revolution, people being killed every day and Homs being destroyed, yet here in Aleppo people were going to the cinema, or for picnics, and constructing big buildings as if nothing had changed. It didn't make sense.

One good thing anyway. Around that time I stopped having asthma attacks.

5

A City Divided

Aleppo, 2012

People say that history is written by the victors, but here is something I don't understand. Why is it we always glorify the bad guys? Even though they have done terrible things we talk about them being charismatic or brilliant military leaders. When I was learning to read and write, Third Sister Nahra made me write out sentences in Arabic over and over again and one of them was 'Alexander is a great hero.' Later I found out he was a selfish, spoilt boy and I felt deceived.

I hate the fact that I didn't know anything about the good people but everything about the bad people. I don't really know anything about the lives of Gandhi or Nelson Mandela. I hadn't heard of Mandela till the World Cup was in South Africa – so why do I know so much about Stalin and Hitler?

I can tell you for example that Hitler was born on 20 April 1889, his father was Alois and his mother Klara, and she died of breast cancer and he was terribly affected. Then he wanted to be an artist but was rejected twice by the Vienna Academy of Fine Arts, and he thought the majority of the selection committee were Jews – so the Holocaust began like that. And he was in love with his niece Geli who killed herself when he left her, and then with Eva Braun who committed suicide with him in a bunker in Berlin.

Stalin killed 6 million people in his gulags and in the Great Terror. Hitler's regime was even more murderous – 11 million people were killed and 17 million became refugees. But it's Stalin and Hitler I can tell you about, not any of their victims. In fifty years is it going to be the same with Assad? People will remember all about him and not the good people of Syria. We will just be numbers, me and Nasrine and Bland and all the rest, while the tyrant will be engraved in history. That is a scary thought.

When the revolution finally came to Aleppo in spring 2012, it was as if everyone had been asleep and had woken up. Like that moment in the morning when the light streams through the apartment and highlights all the dust and cobwebs.

Nasrine was happy that the first people who protested were the students at the university. On 3 May she had gone to her physics class and found a big demonstration under way demanding that Assad go. She and her friends joined in, and it was exciting protesting for the first time in their lives, saying things they had never been able to say before. Then suddenly they heard a bang and the next thing Nasrine knew her eyes were full of tears and burning, so she ran. There was a lot of fear because we knew what kind of regime we had – if anyone got arrested they were certainly dead and maybe their whole family too.

That night Nasrine got a message from a friend who lived in college to say security forces had stormed the dormitories. They shouted through megaphones that everyone should leave, then fired teargas and bullets to disperse them. When some of the students protested and refused to come out, they fired on them and four were killed. Later that night images appeared on Facebook of a dead student, his shirt drenched in blood, and of a dormitory on fire.

The students were of course outraged, and when a delegation of United Nations observers arrived from Damascus to see what had happened, they came out in even bigger demonstrations, maybe 10,000 students, and streamed the rally live on the internet so that everyone could watch. The next day, after Friday prayers, they took to the streets again, holding up pictures of the dead under the words 'Heroes of Aleppo University'. Over and over came the chant 'Assad out!' and 'The people want to topple the regime,' the slogan used in Egypt.

Yaba had told Nasrine not to go. 'What, do you think that a few students will make this regime roll over?' he asked.

'They will roll over you instead.' But I knew she would go. She came back very quiet and she didn't go again. I know my family were selective in what they told me as they thought I wouldn't be able to cope, but I found out later that many people had been beaten and forced to kiss posters of Assad. Nasrine herself had seen one of the students dragged away, a second-year architecture student called Ibrahim who was grabbed by security forces and tortured to death with electric sticks. The boy was from Hama. Many of the demonstrating students were from Hama and had lost parents in the massacre of 1982.

Also, in her department was a boy so smart everyone called him Pythagoras. He disappeared and when he came back he was all in bandages, even his face a different shape, and the authorities wiped out his grades so he had to repeat a year.

But the protests didn't stop. Girls and boys who had only cared about music, clothes, studies and their friends now found themselves trying to bring down a dictator. The university was split with half the professors supporting the revolution and half with the regime. The head of the university protected the student protesters, so a week later he was removed and replaced by a regime supporter. In the end all opposition professors were kicked out. The students were split too. Girls and boys who had been friends were now reporting on one another. In Nasrine's physics class of sixteen, they were divided into two sides, while the Kurds had their own side as they couldn't trust anyone.

Apart from demonstrating, some students were volunteering, taking supplies to protesters and sending out reports on social media. Makeshift field clinics were set up to treat demonstrators, because if they went to government hospitals they might be arrested and killed. It was very risky. In June a burnt-out car appeared in an eastern suburb of Aleppo called Neirab inside which were found three charred and mutilated bodies. One had a gunshot wound and his hands tied behind his back, and his arms and legs had been broken. The corpses turned out to be students – Basel, Mus'ab and Hazem – two medical students and an English student who had been giving first aid to injured protesters and been picked up by Air Force Intelligence a week earlier.

Even though my family didn't tell me things, once I saw pictures of a boy whose head had been cut off lying on a street with a bloody stump where his head should be. When the wind blew in the right direction I fancied I could hear the sound of protests chanting over and over like a drumbeat. Ayee and Yaba were always like tightly strung instruments until Bland and Nasrine came back through the door.

The main protests were in the east of the city. The west was under the tight control of the regime. In Sheikh Maqsoud scary new figures appeared on the streets. These were what we called *shabiha* which means ghosts, criminals paid as paramilitary by the regime to stop people going to protests and make us feel there were eyes everywhere.

We admired the revolutionaries and like them wanted change, not wanting to be ruled by the same family for more than forty years, but mostly we wanted to stay alive. Mustafa said the revolution was interesting for people aged seventeen to twenty-one but not for people like him who were older and working to earn a living for their families. He also told us that some people in Kobane had been given money to go to the demonstrations. Nasrine had a pro-revolution song on her phone and, remembering what she had said to Yaba about who would look after me if they died, I worried that maybe my brothers and sisters would have done more if they hadn't had to think about me. Sometimes when I look back on those days, I wish I had been older at the time and able to make a difference. All I could do was listen to the protest songs. I didn't even get to tear down an Assad poster!

As we had seen elsewhere in Syria, where there was revolution there soon followed war. Assad had stepped up military action and at the beginning of the year had really concentrated force on the central town of Homs, like he was making an example of it, his forces raining mortars and artillery fire on rebel strongholds and bombing centuries-old buildings to dust with people inside. Children were killed, foreign journalists were killed, and the town kept under siege, trapping without food, water or medicines those families who hadn't fled.

Though the regime eventually pushed the rebels out, many other Syrians were revolted by the way they had done it. Like the Aleppo students, people felt they couldn't stay quiet any more. Instead of being cowed, more cities joined the fight.

Mustafa said that Assad was losing swathes of Syria as he concentrated on holding Damascus, Homs and the two coastal provinces on the Mediterranean, and that the rebels were taking much of the countryside. They had also captured border crossings with Turkey and Iraq. But it was at a high cost. Maybe 10,000 people had been killed. He told us people were buying gold sovereigns because they worried that the Syrian pound would become worthless.

Yaba clacked his worry beads and said it was only going to get worse. As front lines hardened into stalemate, the rebels got hold of more effective weapons, some seized from Syrian army bases and others smuggled from Turkey, Jordan and Lebanon and funded by Qatar and Saudi Arabia, while Assad was backed by Russia, China and Iran. It was clear that the rest of the world wasn't going to stop him.

Our war started during Ramadan – the fasting month when everyone becomes tetchy – in the heat and dust of July 2012. It happened quite suddenly. Almost overnight the rebels poured into Aleppo from the countryside. Initially they made quick gains, seizing control of districts in the north-east, south and west within days. Our neighbourhood, Sheikh Maqsoud, was under the control of Kurdish militia, the YPG.

But the offensive was not decisive and it left the city divided. The rebels controlled the east and the regime forces the west, some parts changing hands daily. Soon fighting even reached the gates of the Old City.

We were scared. With the FSA inside the city, the regime would send in its tanks. Also people were a bit unsure of the FSA as all sorts of groups had joined, including criminal gangs. My eldest brothers Shiar and Farhad, who were watching what was going on from Europe on YouTube and Facebook, kept calling and telling my parents, 'Just go, leave this miserable place Aleppo, it's dangerous!'

On streets where rebels had not taken over, the *shabiha* appeared and at once spread terror. Often people fled when the *shabiha* came, which was the idea. Some of our neighbours told stories in hushed voices about them raping women which I wasn't supposed to hear. I worried about Nasrine. The university was in a government-controlled area but had become a centre for anti-government protests and many people took refuge there. It became impossible for Nasrine to go to her classes because to get there she had to cross the front line, so she stayed at home.

As the fighting went on we worried that Bland would be conscripted. Of all my brothers only Mustafa had done his military service. Shiar and Farhad had sought asylum overseas, while Bland had been able to put his off because of university. With the war, Assad's troops were finding themselves thin on the ground, unable to fight on so many fronts.

As a result they were bringing in fighters from their old ally Hezbollah and stepping up conscription. Only those with connections and lots of money could avoid it. On Syrian TV the soldiers were shown as heroic beings, but we all knew that joining Assad's army would mean killing women and children. We prayed we wouldn't become their victims.

The noise wouldn't go away. I tried covering my ears and turning up the volume on the TV but nothing could block out the buzz of the helicopter gunships as they flew to bombard rebel areas followed by the tuk-tuk-tuk of the firing.

Sometimes I was alone when it started, my family out at work or studying or shopping. On the fifth floor of 19 George al-Aswad Road, I watched *Days of Our Lives* and tried not to think what would happen if a bomb struck and the floor crumbled away beneath me. What use would all my information be then? I had so much to do, so many more things to know, I didn't want to die. Even though I'm a Muslim and we believe in destiny, I didn't want to go before doing all that.

Assad could not afford to lose Aleppo, so he had resorted to deploying helicopter gunships and jets, which we could hear flying overhead like angry bees to drop their deadly cargo. As they had done in Homs, his idea seemed to be to devastate a rebel district with artillery fire or bombs, seal off the ruins and force the rebels to surrender. To start with, the bombs were quite far away but then they started zoning in on a neighbourhood near us called Bustan al-Basha which the FSA controlled. Our YPG hadn't let in the FSA, but everyone was saying they would soon get in to Sheikh Maqsoud, and then the regime would start bombing us too.

Can birds sense bombing coming? It felt like it. Birds would stop singing and the air go taut and still as if time had stopped, then came the buzzing as the planes flew over, again and again. Once I saw a documentary that said honeybees can be trained to sniff out explosives – how weird is that?

When the raids started people would rush to basement shelters, but of course I couldn't. My family wouldn't leave me, so we all sat there on the fifth floor as sometimes the building shook and the windows rattled, everyone trying not to look scared. Often I cried, but I was allowed to because I was the youngest and disabled.

Once the bombers had gone, my siblings would go to the balcony where we could see columns of grey smoke rising from the shelling. I went once but not again. It was an awful feeling, to know that in those places people were almost certainly dead, families like ours buried under concrete. It was a feeling mixed with relief that it wasn't us. Is that wrong? I hoped that whoever had taken Sriaa the tortoise was protecting her.

Soon there was another sound too – that of hammering. Other people in our block had started leaving, and before they went they hammered metal sheets over their doors as they were worried about looters. Those with money and passports were flying, others travelling by road to Damascus or the countryside or out of the country to Lebanon where many had relatives and where there were camps for those who didn't.

Every day we heard of more and more acquaintances who had left. Shiar and Farhad kept calling, urging my parents to flee, but Yaba feared that the roads out would be blocked. Of all of us my father was most affected by the bombing. Yet he said his worst fear wasn't the aerial bombing but the army tanks he expected would come into the city.

Eventually my parents agreed that we would leave. The plan was to go back to the Hill of Foreigners in horrid Manbij, which had been liberated by the FSA on 20 July – the first major town to come under rebel control. I remember that day, my mum saying we would spend the Eid feast there in our old house in Manbij because it was Ramadan and then we would return, but I had the feeling she said that just because I needed to be told and that actually we would never come back to Aleppo. What was the choice though? The bombing became so intense that for the last three nights before our departure we were sleepless, and I thought we might actually die.

I didn't like the bombing but I didn't want to go back to Manbij with the cats and dogs. Our last meal in Aleppo was pizza. Because it was Ramadan we could only eat after sunset – what we call *iftar*, our fastbreaker. I didn't fast – those disability benefits again – but the rest of my family did. I had mushroom pizza which is my favourite. While we were eating my sister Jamila called and said, 'Do you know what, a helicopter just bombed Manbij. Maybe this is not the best place to come.' I was happy to hear that as I thought my parents would change their mind and save me from going to that terrible place, but they didn't.

We left on Friday 27 July 2012, the eighth day of Ramadan, with the regime bombing the next-door neighbourhood, and I didn't know then that I would never see my home again. The last thing I did was watch the sports news on TV, then brush my hair. We didn't put metal over our entrance. Ayee simply watered the plants, left the windows open and locked the door. I didn't look back.

Afterwards I would wish I had left some mark of me that someone might find in years to come, maybe like a list of my top-ten favourite geniuses (number one, Leonardo da Vinci), so people could know that once there had been a girl who couldn't walk but knew a lot.

Mustafa had arranged a mini-bus to take me, Bland, Nasrine and my parents. There wasn't much room and we were pretending it was just temporary, so we took only some clothes, the laptop, a few photos and important documents, and of course the TV. As we drove out of the city we saw buildings half collapsed into rubble, almost as if they had crumbled. The roads were packed with hundreds of people leaving. It looked like the whole city of Aleppo was terrified and fleeing to the countryside, literally leaving their breakfast on their tables.

We had to travel through several checkpoints, first those of the regime at the edge of the city, then those of the rebels. At the regime ones I held my breath, worried that they would find Bland, discover he hadn't done his military service and take him away. Because of the checkpoints and all the other vehicles, the 56-mile journey took us three hours instead of the usual one and a half. But we had got out just in time. My aunt and uncle who left a day later took seven and a half hours.

We didn't know what Manbij would be like under control of the FSA. It was kind of like an experiment for Syria. As we drove into the town we saw some banners proclaiming Freedom and a man in a Che Guevara T-shirt, but otherwise nothing looked very different.

Our house looked just the same, and I was not happy to be back there with the family of evil white and orange cats on the roof and the scary black tree. The cat gang had multiplied and the biggest one had a sort of growth on its throat and was even scarier. It was summer and terribly hot in the house, so we slept on the roof. I cried a lot that first night and prayed to God he would stop the fighting and we could go home. The only good thing was to see the stars again. The stars and the beauty of silence. Even Assad couldn't mess with those.

As the Ramadan moon got bigger, you could make out dark and light patches that were its seas and mountains. I remembered all the documentaries I had watched about space and astronauts. 'I wonder what Neil Armstrong would have seen and felt up there on the moon,' I said to Ayee. 'Just sleep,' she grumbled. It was hard to sleep as I was being plagued by mosquitoes which seemed to think I had the sweetest skin. Glad someone likes me! I was covered in bites the next morning and couldn't stop scratching as I watched the opening of the Olympics on TV from London. I was excited to see the Queen. There was even a video with the Queen meeting James Bond. I would be so nervous if I met the Queen.

I was still cross to be in Manbij. But actually we were lucky. The week after we left, the regime started using barrel bombs on Aleppo. These are literally barrels filled with shrapnel or chemicals dropped from a big height by helicopters, that exploded and caused appalling injuries for miles around quite indiscriminately. A lot of the fighting was round the Old City. After hundreds of years of peace and tourists, the citadel was turned into a working fortress again by the regime forces. They used the medieval walls as barriers and the old arrow slits for gun placements and set up snipers' nests in the towers and gun placements.

The souk and covered bazaar had become a front line. My sisters used to love going there and had told me about its miles and miles of magical lanes where you could buy anything from its famous soap to the finest silks, linger in its baths or sip tea and swap stories in its tiled caravanserai. Once I gave Nasrine all the money I had saved from Eid festivals and birthdays and she bought me a gold chain there which was the most precious thing I owned. Now it had become a place where rival snipers trained their rifles and shells fell almost every afternoon. In September we saw on TV that the ancient souk had been set on fire. Hundreds of years of history burnt down.

By the end of 2012 it seemed like the Battle of Aleppo would never end. It was a full-scale war where on one side there was Assad and Hezbollah and on the other all sorts of rebel groups including criminal gangs and Jabhat al-Nusra (also known as the al-Nusra Front), which is the al-Qaeda branch in Syria. Every neighbourhood had become a fiefdom controlled by a different rebel group. The regime was obliterating entire districts while the opposition had cut off nearly all supply routes into the city.

It was better to be in the western part, which was under control of the regime. We heard from friends and relatives still there that in the east there was no fuel to cook with and that the trees in the parks had been stripped of their bark and branches. To get food they had to wait in long bread queues which sometimes got bombed, and families were even scouring rubbish dumps for scraps like you see in poor African countries.

Some people thought Doomsday was coming as forewarned by our Prophet.

6

A War of Our Own

Manbij, Summer 2012

I was watching a programme about the bombing of Dresden and Ayee was getting annoyed. 'Why do you keep watching those old war movies?' she asked. 'We are in a war of our own.'

'One day, in fifty or a hundred years, everyone will read about our war,' I replied.

I liked learning about the First and Second World Wars. I couldn't believe that Gavrilo Princip who shot dead Archduke Franz Ferdinand and so started the First World War was a Serbian teenager aged just seventeen. Thanks, Gavrilo, for ruining the world!

Then the power went off. This was annoying as it was almost time for *Masterchef*, the American version, which had become very exciting as one of the contestants was a blind girl from Vietnam called Christine Ha and I wanted her to win. How could she cook like that blind? It made me think that people need to be in the right place at the right time to shine. Like Lionel Messi was this tiny boy everyone made fun of because of his growth hormones, and now he is the best footballer in the world. I wasn't sure I was in the right place.

Maybe if I was somewhere else, I could be like that fifteen-year-old American boy who invented a way to detect pancreatic cancer, after a close friend died of it. I want to be useful – feeling you are doing nothing is awful. But I do believe everyone is in this world for a purpose. I just hadn't found mine.

Since the war started we were always having power-cuts. Manbij was not as bad as some places as we had the dam near by. But we had rationing and some days there was no power, some days no water. We got used to filling everything with water when we had it. At night the street was completely dark because there were no streetlamps. Every house was full of candles and torches. When there was no power and no TV, there was nothing to do but listen to the war. I could hear everything, the thrum-thrum-thrum of the aircraft then the tuk-tuk-tuk of the guns.

'Why did you bring us here?' I complained almost every day. We had fled Aleppo to escape the war but it had come to Manbij as the regime tried to oust the FSA by bombing them. A high school near us was used as an FSA headquarters, so they bombed the area a lot. It made no sense to me what we had done. The silhouettes of the jets in the sky looked like Second World War dive-bombers from the old movies, and attacked in the same way, the pilots diving steeply before reaching their target, dropping their bombs then pulling up sharply. Afterwards there would be nothing about these raids on Syrian state TV.

During our first week back, one of our stupid neighbours got his rifle out and stood on the roof trying to shoot down the planes. 'Are you mad?' my mum screamed at him. 'If the regime see your gun they will think there are FSA here and kill us all.' She could be scary.

We became experts on weapons. From their sound we could tell the difference between MiG-21 or MiG-23 fighters and helicopter gunships, and between bombs and cluster bombs and missiles. Bland would always go outside or on to the roof to watch and Yaba would be shouting at him to come in.

One day around midday, Nasrine had gone to visit Jamila when the bombing started. I had been watching a fascinating documentary called *Getting to the Moon*, so when I heard the hum of the helicopter overhead, I couldn't believe it. It was like, Assad, are you challenging me? I wanted to keep watching but it became louder and louder. It was a missile bombardment. Every time one struck we felt the room vibrating. Ayee and I hid in the bathroom because it had the strongest ceiling with a layer of cement over the mud roof. Our other refuge was under the concrete step at the front of the house, but that was hard for me to get into.

We were in that bathroom for four hours. If we were all going to die, I wanted it to be me. The rest of my family each had a definite use but I couldn't see I had a use for anybody. Ramadan and Eid had come and gone and we had not gone back to Aleppo as promised. 'You deceived me!' I shouted at Ayee after that. 'We're never going back, are we?'

Another night we were in the house, Yaba praying and Ayee and me just sitting because there was a power-cut and the windows were all open because we couldn't use the fans. Suddenly a warplane came and bombed the street just behind our house. Everything shook and bits of cement and mud flew off the wall, and the gates and windows were all smashed.

'Cluster bombs,' said Ayee. I was so scared I lay on my back with mouth open and looked as if I was dead, so she lay down next to me with her arms around me. Then another plane started roaming around, passing and repassing. I couldn't bear it. 'Go away, plane!' I shouted. 'Away, away, away!' Ayee's phone started ringing. Nasrine was watching from the roof of Jamila's home and could see the bombs landing right by our house. She was terrified.

Finally the planes flew away. When the power came back I turned up the TV and watched a Turkish drama series called *Samar* while Ayee got a broom and swept up the broken glass and rubble.

* * *

Next day we discovered they had bombed a funeral on the street behind, killing five people and injuring dozens. The blast was so powerful that a woman's leg was blown off into the tree. Our neighbours told us that a local spy had called the regime and said there were important people at the funeral. They weren't – they were just ordinary people like us trying to live their lives. Now the funeral had turned into five more funerals.

After a while we got so used to the bombing that one day I realized I couldn't remember normal any more. Unlike Nasrine and Bland who rushed to the roof, I didn't want to watch the bombing because I knew it would leave a scar on my psyche. I had seen programmes about psychology and I didn't want to be turned into a sociopath or a serial killer. My siblings didn't seem to worry about such things.

Nasrine even tried to keep up her studies and insisted on going back to the university in early 2013 for a physics paper. We were really worried as the university had been bombed on the first day of exams in January. She prayed the traveller's prayer the night before and it took her seventeen hours to get there as she had to do a huge circle to avoid the front lines. The mini-bus that took her was driven by a volunteer who called ahead to find out which places to avoid, and when they got into Aleppo from the east on Tariq al-Bab Street they then had to go south and from there to the west to circle the Old City where the main fighting was. Even so she had to cross a line at the end, passing first an FSA checkpoint then one from the regime with a sniper alley in between. As she ran across she saw four bodies lying there which no one could pick up because of the snipers, so they were being eaten by dogs. After that she never talked about going back to Aleppo again. And, by the way, she never got the result of her test.

Nobody really knew who was in charge in Manbij. In the centre of town was a building called the Serai where the courts had been and where the mayor and police all had offices. Those regime officials and police had either gone or defected to the rebels, and now there was a Revolutionary Council made up of engineers, clerics, a pharmacist, a chain-smoking former intelligence officer, a lawyer, a tile manufacturer and a poet who had been in jail for fifteen years.

Some things were good. The shops were open, even the gold merchants, and two independent newspapers had been started, one of which was called the *Streets of Freedom*. It was full of anti-Assad news and a cartoon strip which called him 'Beesho' or 'baby Bashar'. We had never seen such a thing.

What wasn't good were all the armed militants who drove around town. Bland said there were forty-seven different brigades. The main one was led by a commander who called himself Prince and drove around in a white Toyota Hilux pickup full of armed men. He was a short man with a thick neck who before the war had been a petty criminal and had become powerful in the revolutionary chaos by kidnapping rich people, taking their money, then using it to buy cars and weapons for his followers. Mustafa told us that he had gone to the owner of a petrol station who used to hoard fuel and stolen 20 million Turkish lire from him.

All the brigades painted their names on the sides of their pickups but then covered them with mud for camouflage so as not to be bombed by the regime jets. Sometimes they would fight among themselves, and one day there was a big gun-battle between two tribes after men from one tribe kidnapped people from the other. At night local people formed groups to protect their own blocks.

The Assad regime were of course angry to have lost Manbij and if they couldn't have it, it seemed like they wanted to make sure the rebels couldn't either, like children destroying each other's toys. So they bombed our water pipelines, grain silos and administrative buildings. We are people, remember, not toys! The rebels had nothing to fight back with against airstrikes. Also they had no money to run the town. I suppose it was officially chaos because there was no government, so if you were divorcing, getting married, having a child, there were no papers, nothing got registered. And there were no schools working.

People complained that they had no water and weren't getting their pensions any more. Also the regime had cut off our internet, which was very annoying for people like me looking for information. The only reason we had electricity was because we were near the dam, which provides power to a large part of Syria and if our supply was cut, then the rebels might bomb the whole thing.

Fuel was smuggled in but it was very expensive. There were lots of clothes and appliances in the bazaar which people said had been looted from all the homes people had fled in Aleppo, so we never bought any, even though we were kind of camping in our house as we had left almost everything behind. What if our own belongings appeared there? What we did need was bread, and there were long lines of people at the bakeries.

The other problem with war is you had no idea what might happen to you. One day Nasrine and Ayee had gone to the bazaar, heading for their favourite clothes shop to buy something for a wedding. On the way they passed another shop where a long jacket in the window caught Nasrine's eye. Ayee wanted to get on but Nasrine can be stubborn, so they stopped for her to try it on. She had just put it on when they heard the planes followed by an explosion. The place they had been heading towards had been bombed and three people killed, including the owner of that shop. 'That jacket saved our lives,' said Nasrine afterwards. Later she found out that an old schoolfriend of hers, Evelin, had been shopping there and both her legs were blown off and her husband killed.

It wasn't just the bombing that was a problem. Mustafa drives maybe 1,300 miles a week bringing in his trucks, and he said before the revolution that you could sleep in the desert and nobody would touch or steal anything. Now he said that had changed. The FSA checkpoints had all started demanding money – sometimes thousands of dollars – for him and his driver to come through. He started travelling at night and on small roads rather than highways to avoid the checkpoints, but that wasn't always enough.

Not long after we moved back to Manbij, Mustafa was robbed of $21,000 by some members of Jabhat al-Nusra. He had bought some cars from Homs and driven them across the country to Kobane with his driver to sell them. That night when they stopped at a place to sleep, he noticed the driver talking on the phone a lot. The next day the driver said he had heard there was fighting on their planned route, so they should go a different way through a village near Deir al-Zour in eastern Syria. When they got there, they were ambushed by four cars of armed men who started shooting at them and accused Mustafa of working for the PKK, the Kurdish militia. They took all the money he had made selling the cars. After that he sacked that driver as he was sure he had colluded with the gang.

Another time, a few months later, he was robbed by some other militants when he drove into a place called al-Hasakah where there was fighting going on between two villages. Some armed men stopped him and demanded, 'Are you Kurdish?' They told him he must wait for their 'emir', then took him and his driver to a school building where they were holding some other Kurdish people. There, they took his vehicles – two Mercedes-Benz trucks – and stripped him of all his cash – which was about three or four hundred dollars – and his mobile phones before eventually releasing him.

Mustafa didn't tell our father any of this at the time because Yaba would have stopped him working and we relied on Mustafa for money. Mustafa always said war was good for business because the breakdown of order meant you didn't need import licences and because there was more demand for vehicles from all the militias. But his driver used to carry a box of beer with him as he was afraid. Yaba was always warning him, 'You mustn't be too greedy because it will harm you.'

We did have some big family news. Maybe to keep my parents quiet about the dangers of his driving around, at the age of thirty-seven Mustafa suddenly agreed to get married after ten years of saying no to every girl Ayee proposed. The lucky girl was a cousin of ours called Dozgeen living in the village near Kobane. Why he agreed on her and not the others, who knows. I just thanked God I wouldn't have to cover my ears any more as they argued about it. The only annoying thing was that there would be another wedding and crowds of people in the house, which I didn't like.

When Mustafa and my father went to Kobane to meet the girl's family and agree the engagement, how much dowry etc, they got stopped at an FSA checkpoint where the commander demanded money. The man recognized them so took $1,500 – Mustafa said otherwise he might have demanded $5,000. Actually it was lucky because he was carrying gold bracelets, rings and necklaces for the dowry and if the commander had found that he would have taken them all.

In those days people were always coming to our house, refugees like us fleeing Aleppo or other cities. They came and drank tea and crunched pistachios and each told the story of their own migration, how they ran away. I had to turn off the TV when they came which was annoying, but that's not the only reason I hated it. After they left I cried and my mum asked why. 'It's like everyone has opened their own channel and is broadcasting migrant news,' I said. 'Don't be upset,' she replied. 'The most important thing is we are together and nothing has happened to us.'

Her sister, my aunt Shamsa, and her husband Uncle Bozan, whose daughter Azmar had studied law with Nahda and then married my brother Farhad in England, had also left Aleppo and moved next door with their other children. Uncle Bozan was an olive-oil dealer and they had been rich in Aleppo with a nice house but had left everything behind apart from their nice car. 'All I want is for my children to be safe,' my aunt said.

One day in March 2013, Uncle Bozan and their son Mohammed had to go to Damascus to get some documents so that Mohammed could study abroad. Just outside Manbij they were stopped by an armed group who pointed guns at their car and made them get out. They seized Mohammed and told my uncle to go and get 2 million Syrian pounds then they would release him.

Uncle Bozan came back to Manbij in a terrible state. Everyone was trying to raise the money. On the third day Jamila had come to be with Aunt Shamsa, and Nasrine opened the door to go and join her when she exclaimed loudly. Cousin Mohammed was walking down the street. He said the armed group had taken him to a place somewhere in the desert between Hama and Homs where there was a local tribal sheikh who was angry and told them to let him go.

In early 2013 Assad's forces raised the stakes and started firing huge Russian Scud missiles into residential areas of Aleppo. Even more people fled. It seemed to me there couldn't be any people left in Aleppo. You can only imagine how many names we recognized in the list of dead people, especially Nasrine. She was always like 'Oh I know her or him.' Once she cried because a Scud bombed the block of her best friend Wedad in Aleppo and she thought she must be dead. For ages, her friend's phone just rang out and we imagined the worst. Finally a day later she called. She had survived but the block was destroyed and many people died.

I knew we weren't going back to Aleppo. After we'd been in Manbij about six months my parents went back to get our stuff. Yaba didn't want to go, but we Kurdish women are very strong and Mustafa joked that my father was more afraid of my mother than of the war. When they got there they found dust and rubble everywhere and our building was the only one still standing. In our building every window was broken except for ours which Ayee had left open. It was like a ghost town, they said.

Not long after that, in April, we heard that regime jets had dropped chemicals on Sheikh Maqsoud – canisters that exploded and left people foaming at the mouth and narrowed their pupils into pinpricks. Among the dead were two babies.

In some ways I am glad I never went back as I still have the picture in my head of the beautiful city I left behind. Not the bad Aleppo Nasrine and my parents saw. Nasrine says she wished she had never gone back.

Days of Our Lives became a lifeline – the one thing that could make me forget bombing – and I watched it fiercely, glaring at anyone who dared speak while it was on. The rivalry between the Brady and DiMera families seemed more real to me than my own family life. Sometimes I shouted at the screen.

I had been watching *Days of Our Lives* with subtitles. Then one day I realized that I understood one of the English words. The word was 'anything'.

7

Gone with the Wind

In case you think I only know TV, I also liked reading books. Of course I had no way to get them myself, so I had to borrow them from Nasrine or sometimes steal them from her shelf when she was out. Just before we moved to Manbij she got *Gone with the Wind* from Jamila's grown-up stepson (I forgot to mention that Jamila's husband has two wives which I was a bit shocked about when I found out, even though my grandfather has four as is allowed in our culture).

That became my favourite book. Margaret Mitchell is just a genius because through the whole novel you are thinking something will happen between Scarlett O'Hara and Ashley who she is pursuing, then suddenly the scoundrel Rhett Butler shows up and turns out to be the main character and the whole story is actually about Rhett and his love for her, so I'm like what! I love the twist, someone is the bad guy then turns out to be the main character the story revolves around. Also, like us in Syria, Scarlett is trying to survive in the middle of a civil war and keep the home she loves.

The good thing about the books was you could read them by torch or candlelight, and it didn't matter when there was no electricity. The bad thing was there never seemed to be any characters in wheelchairs. Well, only the rich friend Clara in *Heidi*, and Clara ended up walking anyway.

Though I love *Gone with the Wind*, Scarlett is the last person I would like to be. She is beautiful with a teeny waist but vain and spoilt. I don't blame her for her behaviour. She was an inexperienced child and when she wanted something – Ashley – and couldn't have him, she decided to seek revenge for her wounded ego. Some people think it's a weakness for women to follow their heart, but personally I am glad to belong to the gender that gives all they have without expecting anything in return. Of course, we don't really have love marriages in our culture, so we don't have Scarlett's problem. Mostly we marry our cousins to keep all property in our family, though sometimes I worried who would agree to marry me, being disabled.

Around the same time Nasrine got *Love in the Time of Cholera* by Gabriel García Márquez, which both of us loved, and I kept snatching it from her stuff whenever she went out. She was cross, but what she could do? Like I say, disability benefits.

I spent my fourteenth birthday reading that book. It was the first time I hadn't celebrated a birthday with cake and sweets, but I didn't like it at all in Manbij so I refused to celebrate. Also there's something not right about celebrating a birthday in a war. The only good thing – but it was also scary – was I would be meeting my eldest brother Shiar for the first time. He called a few days before New Year's Eve to say he was coming back to Syria to make a film. I was a little bit nervous. What if I didn't feel the way I was supposed to about a brother, and what if he didn't like me or found me strange? I wasn't sure if he really knew to what extent I couldn't walk. Since we left Aleppo I of course had no more treatment and my legs had got worse again. Also I never liked our house being crowded and now there would be even more people coming to see the famous film-maker.

The house got very busy, my mother and sisters making preparations. Mustafa had managed to get a turkey despite the shortages of the war, and that was cooked on the first day as we waited for Shiar to arrive. I was preparing myself for the big moment. The one thing I didn't want to do was get emotional – I didn't want to cry. But when Shiar walked through the door and hugged me, *he* cried.

I soon forgot all my worries about how to behave in front of Shiar because he looked and acted like a member of the family. People came to see him, and after they left we would stay up until like 3.30 a.m. talking. Those were happy times. I had never had three brothers at home. All that was missing was Farhad, but he was far away in a town called Sheffield in England making pizzas. That's what he does, even though he trained to be a dentist. We imagined Europe to be so rich, but for a while he even lived on the streets.

Shiar was shocked by the bombing and the way we had all got used to it. 'How can you live like this?' he asked over and over. He had come to shoot a new film called *Road to Aleppo*, and Bland was going to be in it. Bland, a movie star! They drove around looking for locations and one day went to visit his old school in the west, then on to the Cultural Centre as Shiar used to go there a lot as a boy. That's when they first saw the people we later called Daesh. There were about eight of them and they were in black clothes with balaclavas masking their faces and had closed off the street with their pick-ups. On the front of the Centre they had painted the words 'Islamic State'. It was the first time we had heard of them.

As spring came, more of them appeared. We weren't sure if they were the same as Jabhat al-Nusra or different, but they looked similar with their long beards and short trousers. Prince and the other commanders disappeared, and our neighbours were not unhappy about that as they had been harassing people.

The men in black were kind to people to start with. Once Mustafa was eating in a restaurant and some of them came in and even paid for his meal and for the others dining there.

They held *dawa* forums – kind of public meetings – in the town square, where they talked about jihad against the Assad regime and ran tug-of-war competitions. They offered medical services and provided fuel cheaper than we had been buying on the black market. They even organized a cantaloupe-eating contest for children.

Then more foreigners arrived among them, black and blond people, not just Arabs. Billboards appeared bearing odd-sounding slogans like 'Yes to Sharia Rule in Manbij!' They started to say everyone must cover their wife and daughters and began beating women who didn't. They made prisons and they jailed my cousin as he had a tattoo on his forehead: they said, 'You are like a woman,' and forced him to go on a religious course. It was the same with anyone dressed in jeans. As for women, if my mother or sisters went out they had to be totally covered in black.

Shiar's daughter Rawan had come with him, the one who wouldn't play with me when we were little. She was completely European having grown up in Germany, and now had to cover up in a dark hijab. She thought it was funny to start with, but as summer came it was very hot and it was hard to walk if you weren't used to it. She got fed up.

It was scary and confusing. One day Nasrine was bringing me out to Mustafa's car when what we thought was a Daesh pickup passed, then turned round and came back. My hair was uncovered as always and our hearts stopped. 'Sister, sister, is there a man to talk to?' one of them shouted. 'Yes,' she said and called Bland. It turned out they were FSA and wanted to know if we needed a wheelchair. We said no, even though I didn't have one.

Neighbours we had known for twenty years and who had joined the FSA when they came, now joined Daesh. You might think it odd that people just accepted these outsiders telling them what to do, but Bland said the problem was that Manbij was an uneducated town and people were afraid of not being seen as Islamic. 'You can make them believe any superstition. Just say "Allahu Akbar" three times and every-one comes to you,' he said. He was right – Manbij is a back-ward place, where women never had rights anyway. When we lived there before, Nasrine and our cousin had been the only girls who didn't cover their hair at the high school.

In another town called al-Dana which Daesh had moved into around the same time, residents took to the streets in July to protest against the harsh Islamic laws. Around twen-ty-five people were shot dead and two FSA commanders beheaded, their heads placed next to a dustbin in the town centre. How could these people say they were for Islam? There is no religion in the world that lets you kill innocent people.

We realized later they had moved into Manbij and other towns either because they were border crossings (like Jarablus on the Turkish border) enabling them to bring in their people or because (like Manbij itself and al-Bab) they were strategic strongholds on the road to Raqqa, the city which they would make their headquarters. So now we didn't just have to worry about regime bombing, we also had fanatics like those in Saudi Arabia coming after us.

And Assad just got worse. He was getting assistance from the Iranians, who were helping him push back the rebels. They were even bringing in Afghan fighters as mercenaries. In August 2013 he used sarin gas on rebel-held districts in Damascus. It was like Halabja in 1988 all over again. I remember the date, it was 21 August and I had been watching *Days*. When it finished I flipped through the channels and accidentally saw Al Jazeera showing all these dead bodies. It was awful. I used my walker to drag myself to the bathroom and turned on the shower, still wearing all my clothes. When I came out dripping wet I asked Nasrine to make me a coffee, which I am not allowed to drink.

By then Shiar had finished shooting his film and gone back to Germany. He told me the story of the film and asked me what I thought of it. It's about a man who comes back from Germany trying to find his mother in Aleppo. He meets a girl photographer who offers to help him, then they come across a bombed village and when they try to get help for the victims, they end up locked up by the rebels. 'I don't like it because there's no hope in it and we need to believe in hope,' I replied. He started crying. I think it was the wrong thing to say.

More and more people we knew were leaving the country. Some of our cousins and neighbours started to say they wished the revolution had never happened. I didn't agree.

'Would you be happy if you are ruled by the tenth generation of Assads?' I asked them. 'I don't think so.'

Yet in some ways life still went on as if nothing was happening. Around the same time was the wedding of my brother Mustafa. Like I said, I hate my siblings' weddings. Actually my all-time favourite episode in *Days of Our Lives* was the one fans call Black Wedding when my favourite character EJ DiMera – yes he's the bad guy – marries Sami from the rival Brady family.

In case you don't know, EJ is the son of the biggest villain on the show, crime-boss Stefano DiMera. EJ is very handsome and has a British accent because he was packed off to boarding school in Britain – Eton with Prince William! – then Oxford. After that he became a racing driver, but then his father summoned him back to America to make life hell for the Brady family. It was clear EJ would do anything to win his father's love and be part of a family for the first time, but anyone could see really that Stefano was just using him and not capable of love.

To please his father – and infuriate the Bradys – EJ seduces Sami Brady, who is the black sheep of her family. She ends up pregnant and they get married. This is supposed to end the vendetta, only he gets shot in the back by her ex-husband Lucas just after they say 'I do'. That was kind of funny for me as I had thought *Days* was so different to our lives, but in our society we have vendettas – like the one that made us move from Kobane – and we often resolve them by marriage.

In our tradition people often fire guns at weddings to celebrate. I couldn't see what there was to celebrate as weddings meant losing another member of my family. Ayee tried to explain that this time we would be gaining someone – Dozgeen, Mustafa's bride, who was only a few years older than me. They were even going to live in our house to start with, and we would go and stay with our cousins next door. I couldn't see how that was good.

Soon enough Dozgeen was brought from Kobane. She didn't have any wedding dress and it took them four hours to come through small villages because of the fighting. When she arrived I was terribly tired and my stomach was upset, so I just wanted to be left alone, but it was a historic moment in our family. The house filled with guests who stayed until late and did traditional dancing and acted like there was no war or Daesh, and I had to smile all the time as if I was enjoying myself.

Ayee was right. Having Dozgeen was like getting a new sister. The first day after the wedding she was wearing a beautiful purple dress and sat on a chair and I started interrogating her. 'What's your favourite colour? What's your favourite film? Your favourite food?' She answered everything, then she told me her mother had advised her to be nice to me because I was very precious to the family.

*　*　*

It was good to have someone new in the house as my TV kept going off in the power-cuts, which was terribly annoying because every morning I got up desperate for the latest twist in the love affair between EJ and Sami, or EJami as we fans call them.

After EJ gets shot, Sami is forced to pretend to love him to try to help him to recover, then when he does, he has an affair with Sami's arch-rival Nicole and gets her pregnant too. The story of EJ and Sami is basically this explosive love affair where they fight and get together and fight and lie and fight some more. Somehow even though EJ is mean and cruel he is also so fragile and desperate to be loved – and his father so cruel – that you end up rooting for him.

So in addition to all the stress of the bombing and my own family wedding, I had to deal with all the goings-on of this rebellious couple. Sometimes I thought I would go mad.

And I kept missing key episodes, because the show was broadcast on MBC4 from Saturday to Wednesday between 9.15 and 10 a.m. and Manbij's electricity supply was rationed. Some days it would go off at 6 a.m. and come back at 9 a.m. just in time, but other days infuriatingly the power would go off at 7 a.m. and come back at 10 a.m. There was a rerun at 4 p.m., but at that time the living room was often full of guests with their awful migrant news or my father and his friends talking about the situation, so I would miss it. When I couldn't watch *Days* it felt as if I didn't have my friends when I needed them most, even though they had no idea of my existence.

I kept telling my family I couldn't miss any episodes because they were my English lessons. Since discovering I could understand the word 'anything', I had started trying to understand more English. Soon I realized I knew lots of the words and began collecting phrases. I loved it when I could understand whole sentences. The other good thing about Shiar coming to stay had been practising English with him as he spoke it a bit. I didn't know anyone else who spoke it.

I started being more targeted. I watched *Dr Oz*, a programme about health, for medical words, thinking maybe one day I would go to a hospital outside for treatment; *Masterchef* for food and culinary terms; *America's Got Talent* for cultural references; wildlife programmes for names of animals; documentaries for historical and scientific thought which could be useful if I ever went to college (even if I had never been to school!). But general conversation was of course from *Days*. Sometimes these characters seemed more real to me than my own brothers who I rarely saw. I was desperate that their story should end in the way I wanted. Something had to have a happy ending.

8

Forgive Me, Syria

It was Shiar who made us leave Syria in the end. He had been shocked at how we were living with the bombs and the jihadis and had kept on at us ever since he got back to Germany.

That spring and summer of 2014 felt like everything was coming to a head. First we heard that the writer Gabriel García Márquez had died, so Nasrine and I were very upset. Then EJ was killed off in *Days of Our Lives*. He and Sami had finally reconciled, then he was betrayed and killed by his own bodyguard. I guess I had known it was going to happen and was kind of pleased that I had second-guessed the show's writers, but still it left a big hole in my life.

Assad forces had disappeared from our area as they were busy defending Damascus, and now Kurdish militias, YPG, were the ones fighting Daesh. We Kurds are Muslims but we are not obsessed by that – our culture is more how we identify ourselves. People started to talk about our area as Rojavo – our Kurdish state.

In January Daesh set up their headquarters in the town of Raqqa, which was less than 100 miles away. In Manbij they had become stricter. Apart from forcing women to wear niqab, they told men to go to prayers at the mosque five times a day. They had beheaded a boy of fourteen who they accused of raping an old woman, and the mother died of sadness. They also banned music. I had just discovered classical music and adored the Spanish guitar of Rodrigo's *Concierto de Aranjuez* and Andrea Bocelli singing 'Time to Say Goodbye'. Actually I was annoyed: how come I hadn't discovered this before? I thought I was good at discovering things!

In June Daesh caught everyone by surprise by capturing the Kurdish city of Mosul in northern Iraq and marching towards Baghdad. They released a video of their leader Abu Bakr al-Baghdadi giving a sermon from the mosque, proclaiming a caliphate which he said would stretch all the way to Spain. 'This is a duty upon Muslims,' he said. 'A duty that has been lost for centuries and they must always seek to establish it.'

I mean there hasn't been a caliphate for a thousand years. Move on, Baghdadi! And if you are going to take us back in time, ditch the Rolex watch. Anyway it was on all the international news broadcasts, and suddenly everyone in the West seemed to be talking about nothing but Daesh, like they had just discovered them.

One day Nasrine and Bland were in a car driving round the roundabout when they noticed there was a head on a spike. It started happening more and more. Another day gunmen came to the house of Aunt Shamsa and Uncle Bozan, whose son had been kidnapped, and fired in the air then banged on the door – maybe because they had two nice cars outside. No one was home, but as soon as my aunt and uncle came back and heard what had happened they decided to leave and move to Kobane.

Later they called us with a terrible story. Aunt Shamsa told us that their neighbour who was also a Kurd had a beautiful daughter, and one day when her father was not at home militants from Daesh came wanting to take her away. Her thirteen-year-old brother tried to stop them, but they killed him. A day later they returned and said, 'She must marry our Emir. Make her ready tomorrow, and we will collect her.' Her terrified parents had no choice. The men came back and took her, and after a week she was allowed home for a day. Her mother asked her, 'Who is your husband, is he a good man?' The girl started crying. 'You think you let me marry one man?' she said. 'Every night I have ten men.'

The next day our family left.

* * *

103

Only it wasn't our whole family. My parents were staying behind to look after the house. They said they would come soon, but I remembered Ayee's promises when we left Aleppo that we would go back after the Eid holiday, and since then two more Eids had passed. And in my heart I knew they didn't want to leave Syria. Tears ran down my face as we said goodbye. I clung to Ayee. I had never been separated from her before. We had always slept together.

We left in the morning after a breakfast of flatbread dipped in olive oil flavoured with oregano, sumac and sesame seeds, kind of our version of peanut-butter sandwiches. Mustafa had gone ahead to the Turkish town of Gaziantep, where many Syrians were living, to find us an apartment. Uncle Ahmed was driving us in his car as he had a passport, so could cross the border. Bland sat in the front and me, Nasrine and Mustafa's wife Dozgeen, who already seemed like she had always been part of the family, were squashed into the back. There wasn't much room with all our stuff. They were all wearing burqas. It was a beautiful sunny day, and to anyone watching we could have been a normal family on a day trip. The evil white cat with the orange eyepatch and throat tumour was standing on the roof watching us. I wouldn't be sorry to leave them. They were like Daesh cats.

It was less than an hour to the border. Soon we were driving up to the rolling green hills and golden wheat fields beyond which lay Turkey. Our plan was to cross at Jarablus, which is on the west bank of the Euphrates and was also under Daesh control. As we got near we saw their black flag flying. It was the first time I had seen it. I couldn't help remembering the reports from January when there was fighting in Jarablus and Daesh commanders shot people dead and beheaded rebel commanders, sticking their heads on spikes, in the main square. I hoped I wouldn't see anything like that.

Moments later we rounded a bend and saw a roadblock. Men in dark clothes were holding up their guns to stop us. They were scary with their long beards, long hair and short trousers and guns pointing at us. It was like an action movie.

My uncle rolled down the windows. It felt like even the birds had stopped singing.

The militants pointed at me. 'Why isn't she wearing a veil?' they demanded. Their Arabic was strange to us. I was so scared I was quivering.

'She is only twelve,' said Bland, 'and she is disabled.'

The men conferred for a while. Then one of them turned back to Bland. 'Tell the girl to cover her head in future,' they told him, as if I were deaf.

They let us through and we continued. We could see a huge red Turkish flag with its white crescent moon and star the other side. There were hundreds of other Syrians at the crossing point, mostly on foot, with suitcases and bundles of possessions. It was the first time I realized we were refugees.

My uncle, who like Mustafa crossed back and forth bringing in phones for his business, knew one of the border officials, so we didn't have to queue. He said it used to be easy crossing – Turks and Syrians would pop across from one side to the other, the Turks for cheap petrol and cigarettes and us Syrians to buy luxury goods, almost as if there was no border.

Those were the days when Assad and Turkish President Recep Erdoğan were allies and friends. That had changed. Assad had taken no notice of Turkish officials who came to Damascus in the early days of the revolution to try to persuade him to listen to protesters and introduce reforms. When their pleas fell on deaf ears, Erdoğan let the first main opposition group, the Syrian National Council, organize a government in exile in Istanbul, and the FSA have training camps near the border.

Uncle Ahmed slipped the border official a wad of notes, but his contact said only he and I could go through. Bland said he would go and talk to someone. We waited for four hours in the car. The day got hotter. While we were waiting I asked Uncle Ahmed information questions like why the Turkish flag has a moon and a star (he said they came in the dream of the first Ottoman ruler) and what is the population of Turkey compared to Syria (80 million compared to 23 million – well, that was before everyone left). There were children playing near by, and we noticed that they were pretending to shoot and behead each other. What had happened to our country?

When Bland came back he said it was not possible to cross there, but he had heard of another place so he, Nasrine and Dozgeen got a taxi to a village called Arai where smugglers help you cross. They paid $50 each and were put with a group of around twenty refugees. The smuggler told them to walk a little towards the border fence and then hide in the nearby bushes. After about half an hour of waiting he gave them the signal that they could cross. The border was just a small fence that they could easily step over. They walked for about half an hour over the other side to a spot where a van was waiting for them to take them to meet us.

Back at Jarablus, Uncle Ahmed and I simply drove across. It seemed a mundane journey for something that was such a momentous change. On a wall someone had painted 'Your homeland is not a hotel you can check out of if the service is bad'. Tears ran down my face. It was hard to believe Aleppo was only two hours away. I had no friends to say goodbye to and my brother and sister were going to be with me, but I still felt sad. Forgive us, Syria, I whispered.

After picking up Bland, Nasrine and Dozgeen, who were hot and excited after their adventure, we drove for a while along a road parallel to the border. Every so often we saw vast encampments of white tents. Turkey had been welcoming refugees and had provided a number of camps along the border. First a small trickle arrived, then 10,000 in the first year, and now there was a flood. Half a million or more Syrians had crossed the border before us. So many were leaving it felt as if Assad would be left with a country of no people, or just his Alawites. The camps were all full, and we saw people sleeping on the sides of the highway under branches and sheets. I was glad we had a place to go.

The drive to Gaziantep was about three hours. I suddenly felt terribly tired. I was excited to be in a new country, happy to be away from bombs and Daesh, as if a weight had come off us, but I was missing my parents.

We entered Gaziantep as dusk fell. It was a huge town with an imposing stone fortress, and the hills were covered with stone houses in shades of grey, pink and ochre and mosques with shiny gold crescents on top of the minarets. There were lights everywhere. It was so long since we had seen working streetlights. The streets were busy with people out on a Friday night. Our eyes popped at the women in tight jeans and T-shirts or tiny mini-skirts, and the boys and girls out together. There were roads lined with mobile-phone shops and bakeries selling the local baklava sweets and restaurants with tables spilling out on to the pavement. We saw movie theatres, shopping malls, and families in parks. When we opened the windows it smelled of pistachios and rosewater and hookah pipes. 'It's like Aleppo used to be,' said Nasrine.

Our new home was in a suburb called Jinderes in the north of the city, where more of the women were in kaftans and scarves. Bland explained that it was a Kurdish area. A lot of refugees were staying with relatives, but we were lucky to have Mustafa and Shiar to contribute and they had rented us a first-floor apartment on a main street, over a supermarket, with a Syrian kebab shop just a few doors away. Bland carried me upstairs. Only one floor this time, not five. The apartment was light and airy with a large room scattered with cushions for us all to sleep in, and a TV of course. Immediately I started searching for familiar channels like National Geographic, and MBC4 for *Days of Our Lives*.

We also had the internet. I had never used Google before. The first thing I searched was *Days of Our Lives*. Imagine my astonishment to discover it was the longest-running soap opera in America.

The first night Nasrine and I watched a movie about a quiz show in India called *Slumdog Millionaire*. The poor boy is part of a gang he calls the Three Musketeers and is one question away from the big prize. The question is the name of the Third Musketeer and he doesn't know! I realized then that I didn't know the names of the actors playing my favourite characters EJ and Sami. Immediately I Googled them.

I didn't have to wait so long to see my parents in the end. Just fifteen days after we left my mum fell ill in Manbij with a respiratory attack. Mustafa was in the house and took her to hospital. When they got there it was full of men with long beards and long hair in their dark uniforms scaring people. They were only allowing people in who were critically ill, especially those hurt in bombardments. Ayee was struggling to breathe, but they told her there were no doctors and she should leave. The next day Mustafa brought my parents to Gaziantep.

We were all together again, even if it was in a different country. And there was no bombing. 'You know those two years in Manbij felt like ten,' Ayee admitted a few days later.

Yet somehow I knew that Gaziantep wouldn't be the end of the journey. Shiar had mentioned Germany. I didn't tell anyone, but one night when everyone was sleeping I borrowed Shiar's laptop and Googled 'Germany cures for cerebral palsy'.

PART TWO

The Journey

Europe, August–September 2015

To be a successful migrant you need to know the law. You need to be resourceful. You need a smartphone and to be on Facebook and WhatsApp. You need some money. Ideally you know a bit of English. And in my case you need a sister to push your wheelchair.

Nujeen

9

Widen Your World

Gaziantep, Saturday 22 August 2015

It wasn't easy saying goodbye. The night before, Ayee had made my favourite dinner which was a traditional Kurdish dish of turkey with bulgur wheat and parsley – very spicy if you haven't had it. Nasrine counted our money – she had a neck purse with $300 and 1,300 Turkish lire (euros we would get en route) – then checked through our things. She had bought a grey backpack printed with the words Touching Air and in it had packed a change of clothes for us both – a shirt and jeans – as well as pyjamas, underwear, toothbrushes and a charger for her phone which was the most essential item. I also had a walking frame, which was a bit awkward to carry but might be useful for going to bathrooms. It didn't seem very much for such a long journey.

My father was very tearful as he always says family is the most important thing in life. 'Pray for our safe journey, Yaba,' I told him. I didn't want him to come to the airport as I knew he would get too emotional and I don't like people getting emotional.

Only Ayee and Mustafa came to see us off. Before we left my mother took off my gold necklace from Aleppo, which was the only precious thing I had, as we had heard that there could be robbers along the way. She put it round her own neck and started crying. 'Oh God, I am not going to New York or LA, only to Europe,' I told her crossly. Then Nasrine pushed me away, past a big advert for Turkish Airlines proclaiming 'Widen Your World', and I waved goodbye.

I didn't really see it as goodbye. I was sure we would see them again soon. And I was excited. Me, who had spent so many years barely leaving the fifth-floor apartment in Aleppo, now headed all the way to Germany! We would fly west across Turkey to İzmir then across sea and land to Germany to join Bland, who had left four months earlier. I had Googled where he was in Dortmund and it was 1,800 miles as the crow flies, which is an odd expression as crows don't really fly straight, and 2,300 miles by road.

My parents said they were too old to make such a journey, and Mustafa needed to keep earning money to pay their rent and for our trip. So it would be just me and Nasrine. And my wheelchair, which we had recently got from a charity.

We decided to leave because life had stopped in Gaziantep. The Turks might have let us into their country but they didn't like us. Once we had been proud Syrians from an ancient culture. Now we were refugees – nothing. Bland couldn't work, Nasrine couldn't study. On the plus side there were no wild cats and dogs and no bombs or shelling, though if anyone dropped anything or if a car exhaust backfired we jumped. But truly it was pretty miserable for us Syrians in Turkey. On top of that we were Kurds. The only way to work was illegally, and then you were at the mercy of Turkish bosses who took advantage by paying rotten salaries or sometimes nothing.

It was OK for me as I busied myself watching the TV to improve my English (not Turkish, which I thought was a terrible ugly language) and using the internet to get more information. The feeling of getting new information is a beautiful one, and Shiar had lent me a laptop so I could look up anything. It was like a treasure trove. Who invented *Tom and Jerry*? How rich is Mark Zuckerberg? How did Stephenie Meyer come up with the idea of vampires for the *Twilight* books? And most importantly I Googled all about James Scott and Alison Sweeney, the actors playing EJ and Sami in *Days*.

I had also become obsessed with Queen Victoria and how when her husband died she wore black for the rest of her life – and it was a long life, for Albert died when she was forty-two and she lived to be eighty-one.

It's funny because in films she seems very dour, but then I found she had kept all these diaries which you can read online. So I did – though not all 141 volumes! – and it turns out she was not like that at all. Albert was her cousin and a German and she had to propose to him because she was queen. What I liked about her was she became queen so terribly young, just eighteen, and married at twenty, but she didn't lose her foolishness. Even though she was the most powerful person in the world, she wrote in her diary about being madly in love like a teenager, and staring at Albert's 'beautiful face' the morning after their wedding, and how they talked about opera, architecture and exhibitions. I hate it when women give up their true natures; you should be crazy, fall in love, cry over movies and sing in the rain, however powerful you become.

When Albert died of typhoid aged just forty-two, Victoria wrote that she had a 'heavy broken heart'. She never really recovered. I'd never thought that queens could have broken hearts too.

Another interesting fact. Victoria's first name was actually Alexandrina and she was named after the grandson of Catherine the Great, Tsar Alexander I, who defeated Napoleon and was one of my Romanovs.

Oh we needed a mighty queen or a Romanov to deal with all the problems in Syria. You might not know, but many years ago we did have a powerful queen in Syria: she is on our 500-pound banknotes. Her name was Zenobia and she was a descendant of Cleopatra. She was born in the third century AD in Palmyra and like Victoria she became queen very young, in her twenties, and had her own empire, the Palmyrene. She was so audacious she took on the might of Rome, the world's greatest empire, and conquered Egypt and much of what is today Turkey. A woman doing that. Daesh hate her!

We'd spent a year in Gaziantep, but the chances of going back to Syria seemed to be getting more and more remote. Daesh were spreading like a plague. I refuse to call them Islamic State as who said they are a state? Can I just become Nujeen State? Of course not!

Just after we left Manbij in August 2014, they besieged Mount Sinjar where thousands of Yazidis had fled after Daesh massacred hundreds of their people in surrounding villages including children, telling them to convert or lose their heads, and seized hundreds of women to rape and enslave. Seeing those desperate people trapped on the mountain with no food or water finally made the world do something. The US and British helped Iraqi forces airlift the Yazidis off the mountain, and the following month the US and a few Arab countries like Jordan, UAE and Bahrain began airstrikes in Syria. A bit late, Mr Obama.

After the Sinjar massacre, Daesh headed towards Kobane and everyone thought they would do the same there, so the whole city was evacuated, including our sister Jamila and lots of our family. Only Kurdish fighters from the YPG stayed behind. We were watching it on YouTube, everyone queuing up at the border fence with desperate faces like in war movies and their belongings in bags and bundles. We were also on the phone to people there who said it felt like Doomsday. Ayee said she'd dreamt Daesh had taken over the city. Kobane was a Kurdish city and always had been, so it was an awful feeling to have Daesh trying to capture it. I really didn't want something else bad added to our calendar, along with the Halabja massacre. We Kurds are truly the orphans of the world. As I often do in desperate situations, to calm myself I turned to the Koran and my favourite chapter or surah, Yasin, which we call the heart of the Koran and I always find comforting.

Relatives started to arrive from Kobane, including Aunt Shamsa and Uncle Bozan, and soon our apartment in Gaziantep was packed – thirty-six people came to our house. We didn't have anywhere near enough cushions and blankets, so that first night we stayed up talking and it felt homey.

It took almost five months, until January 2015, before Daesh was pushed out of Kobane by the YPG and the US coalition air raids and people could go home. The city had been almost all destroyed in the fighting, but we don't care if only crumbs are left as long as they are not under Daesh control.

A month later, in February 2015, came the worst thing of all – seeing Daesh burn alive a Jordanian pilot they had shot down. They locked the poor man in a cage and set fire to him and videoed the whole thing. And in May they captured our ancient city of Palmyra and beheaded an eighty-two-year-old archaeologist everyone called Mr Palmyra because he knew more about the ruins than anyone. They hung his body upside down with his head on the ground next to it, still wearing his spectacles. Then they started blowing up 2,000-year-old temples and tombs and taking sledgehammers to ancient statues.

As for Assad, he had held elections and got himself re-elected for a third seven-year term. The regime kept bombing. There isn't a good side in this story.

Meanwhile we Syrians caught in the middle kept getting killed. Every family had a tragedy and any time the phone rang you worried. On 25 June 2015 we got a terrible phone call. Aunt Shamsa and Uncle Bozan had also moved to Turkey when Kobane was attacked but had gone back for the funeral of one of their in-laws, the father of the man married to their daughter, my cousin Dilba. He had been killed when he stepped on a landmine left behind by Daesh when they were pushed out of Kobane. My mother had begged them not to go, but Aunt Shamsa insisted, saying this would be her last visit to Syria before leaving for Europe.

But in the early hours of the morning before the funeral, men from Daesh who had shaved off their beards and dressed like our YPG People's Protection Units came into the village of Barkh Botan on the southern edge of Kobane and went from house to house slaughtering people. In every family they left one person alive so they could tell what they had seen. Then they set off three car bombs on the edge of Kobane and cruised around in white cars or on foot killing people as they tried to flee. Snipers on rooftops killed people trying to retrieve bodies from the street.

My uncle and aunt heard the explosions and shooting and fled in their car. They called their son Mohammed and said, 'Daesh are here and we don't know where to go.' Then they called him again, saying with relief they had made it to a YPG checkpoint. That was the last thing Mohammed heard from them. In fact the people at the checkpoint were Daesh and shot my uncle and aunt in the head. Dead, just like that, for nothing. That was the worst day of my life.

Around 300 ordinary people were killed in just that one night. Not surprisingly people just kept leaving Syria. By that August, 4 million Syrians had like us left the country and another 8 million had to abandon their homes, that's like 40 per cent of the whole nation. Most had gone to neighbouring countries like Lebanon and Jordan or Turkey like us, but these places were filling up and people could see this was going to go on for a long time, so around 350,000 had gone on to Europe. A tide of people was on the move and from what we could see on TV and heard on the news, it seemed like the EU couldn't cope. So many people were going that just in the month before we left, the EU had 32,000 asylum applications.

Bland and Mustafa told us if we were going to go, it had to be soon.

The easiest way would be by plane, flying into an EU country then requesting asylum on landing. But you can't get on an international flight without a passport or visa and we had neither.

That left two main ways to go. There was the central Mediterranean route via Libya across the sea to Italy, but that was hazardous. We were envious when Libya got rid of Colonel Gaddafi in 2011, but now it was chaos with militias all fighting each other and the country divided between two or maybe three groups. We heard that foreigners were being picked up by police and thrown into detention centres, where they were beaten and got diseases like scabies. If they did get out and find a smuggler they were often crammed into rickety boats which got shipwrecked. In just one shipwreck in April 2015 around 800 people drowned. The safer option was the Balkan route from Turkey to Greece which was in the EU and because of the Schengen Agreement (we'd found out about that) there were no border controls and you could go from one country to the next without showing a passport.

The easiest land crossing used to be between Turkey and Greece. There is a 128-mile border between the two which runs along a river you could float across, except for 7.5 miles where the border moves away from the river. However, the Greeks have their own problems with their economic crisis and the last thing they wanted was more migrants. So in 2012 they fenced off the short land section with 12-foot barbed wire backed up by thermal cameras and border guards. That meant the only land route left was via Bulgaria, and that was how Bland had gone.

It is just under 100 miles from Istanbul to the Bulgarian border, but the problem was that the last bit was over high forested mountains. People got lost there or froze to death in the winter. Now it was summer, but there was no way of climbing in my wheelchair. Also as the numbers went up the Bulgarian border guards were beating people and setting dogs on them, and sending them back. Bland had paid a people smuggler to help him make the journey, but it still took him three attempts to cross. When he did finally make it he got arrested at a police checkpoint just before Sofia and was kept for eighteen days in jail where they stole some of his money.

It's actually illegal to lock up asylum seekers. The UN Convention on Refugees allows a person fleeing conflict to enter a country without paperwork – only once he or she has been refused asylum can they be locked up. But lots of EU countries had been doing it for years – Malta, Italy and Greece – and nobody did anything.

Conditions in the Bulgarian jail were terrible, but Bland's biggest fear was that he would be fingerprinted. All migrants know about the Dublin regulation, which says a person should request refugee status in the first EU country they arrive in. Once you've touched the inkpad with your fingers and pressed them on paper, you are trapped in that country as it means you have registered a claim there, even unwittingly, and must stay there until authorities of that country either approve the asylum request or send you home. We'd heard of plenty of people stuck in a country they didn't want to be in and which didn't want them either, waiting for the wheels of bureaucracy to slowly turn.

Bland knew he must avoid this, so he paid a bribe not to be fingerprinted and was released. He took a bus to Sofia and stayed three nights with a friend. Bulgaria is the poorest country in the EU and wasn't at all like the wealthy Europe he had imagined. He didn't go out as he didn't want to end up in a Bulgarian camp, where he'd heard that conditions were appalling, with refugees packed into crowded rooms not fit for humans and given little food and only cold water for washing. If you didn't get picked up by police, there was also the risk of being beaten up by thugs from far-right parties who were demanding immigrants out.

Bland's friend put him in touch with a Bulgarian mafioso who charged 1,300 more euros (euros are the main currency of smugglers, though some accept dollars) to take him to a place near the border with Serbia where he was kept in a small room for three days. Then he was woken at 2 a.m. and loaded into the back of a closed food truck with thirty other refugees where they couldn't see and could hardly breathe.

Just as they thought they were going to suffocate, the truck driver stopped and offloaded them in some woods and told them it was a two-hour walk to cross the border. A man in a mask met them to guide them and it was actually fifteen hours through cold rain. Finally inside Serbia, they were handed over to Serbians who drove them to Belgrade. From there Bland was put on a train with three other Syrians headed to a village called Horgoš near the border with Hungary. They were just starting to relax when Serbian police boarded the train and said they would send them back to Bulgaria. Bland and his fellow travellers were desperate to avoid that, so they paid 50 euros each and the police let them go.

When they got to Horgoš, they went to the park as instructed but there was no sign of the smuggler who was supposed to meet them. They waited all night in the park until at 7 a.m. he finally answered his phone. He told them to stay there and a car would come to take them, but it did not arrive till the next day. That car took them to near the border, where police had been paid to let them through, then they paid another 1,500 euros to go to Vienna in a mini-bus. By that time Bland was so suspicious he kept following the journey on Google maps to make sure he wasn't heading back to Bulgaria. From Vienna he took a train to Germany and finally claimed asylum.

The plan was he would get residency in Germany and then send for us through a process called family reunification, which means if one family member gets asylum he or she can send for the rest. But there were so many refugees arriving he was still waiting. Meanwhile we could see on TV that waves of people were going, and we heard from many of our friends that the journey had got easier.

Nasrine was really stubborn and kept saying we should just go before Europe closed its doors, and in the end the family agreed. I never thought it would happen but when it did I was delighted. The question was how. Bland's journey had cost more than 6,000 euros and took over a month with lots of hiking. Me, Nasrine and the wheelchair couldn't do that. Anyway, the Bulgarian route was no longer possible. As the crisis worsened and more refugees surged into Europe, the Bulgarian government wanted the EU to come up with a long-term solution. EU ministers kept having summits and meetings. But all they did really was talk and say how bad it was. The Bulgarians got fed up and decided to copy Greece and build their own fence to keep refugees out.

So now the only way was by sea, across the Aegean to one of the Greek islands like Lesbos, Samos, Kos or Chios. Bland said he had met many people who had done it. On the map it did not look far.

10

In Search of a People Smuggler

İzmir, 22 August–1 September 2015

When I saw where we were sitting on the plane, I started shaking my head violently. Row 14, right in the middle. I had seen so many documentaries about plane crashes and I knew the back was the most secure place. That's why it is where they keep the black box which records all the flight information. The middle was the worst.

'We can't sit in the middle!' I whispered urgently to Nasrine as the steward lifted me into the seat and fastened me in. 'Don't be silly,' she replied. 'We can't move.'

The engines revved beneath us and the stewardess came round with a basket of boiled sweets. The plane moved along Gaziantep's runway and I gripped the arms of the seat. I knew from the documentaries that most crashes take place on take-off or landing. As we took off I closed my eyes and uttered a short prayer. The wheels lifted and it felt like I imagined a rollercoaster in an amusement park would feel. Though I wanted to die in space I didn't want to die beneath the Karman line at the edge of the atmosphere.

When I opened my eyes I saw Nasrine had closed hers. I didn't know till later that she was scared too, and she didn't even have the plane-crash information! Turns out even for someone doing a physics degree and knowing about forces like lift and drag, it doesn't seem very natural to have this huge weight barrelling through the sky.

Once we had taken off without crashing and settled in the sky, I looked outside. Everything was so small down below, people were like ants. Up among all the fluffy white clouds, I felt excited to be on a plane for the first time. The flight to İzmir was just two hours, then it was time to land which was the other really risky part. I tried not to remember all those documentaries. We didn't crash, but my ears were exploding and for ages afterwards I couldn't hear.

Afterwards I felt terribly exhausted and told Nasrine I had jetlag. She said it was impossible as we hadn't crossed any time-zones. We got a taxi and Nasrine kept phoning people. Some of our relatives were already in İzmir, including our elder sister Nahda who had travelled there the previous year with her husband Mustafa and his parents. Sorry, there are a lot of Mustafas in our family!

*   *   *

The taxi took us to a place called Basmane Square, opposite a mosque and a police station. There were Syrians everywhere and merchants with piles of orange life jackets and black inner tubes. Mustafa met us by the newspaper kiosk and took us up one of the surrounding streets, where small huddles of people were sitting on the pavement or at tables, smoking and drinking tea, playing checkers or just waiting. All of them had backpacks by their side, some inside black dustbin bags to protect them from water.

We stopped at a shabby hotel where Mustafa said our sister and relatives were staying in the basement. Some young men lifted me down the concrete steps. The place was a mess – it was packed with people and mattresses and empty biscuit packets. Waiting for us there was Nahda along with their four young daughters from nine-year-old Slav down to baby Helaz, who we had never met, and some of Mustafa's relatives who would travel with us. Mustafa would stay in İzmir because his parents were old and couldn't make the journey, so his nephew Mohammed would look after Nahda (we have a lot of Mohammeds too!).

They had already been there two nights. Someone brought us sandwiches as we were terribly hungry, and while we were eating them, one of our cousins told us that there had been a cat in the basement the previous night. A cat! I freaked out. 'I'm not going to sleep here!' I said. I was so tired and stressed about the cat I didn't notice that a lot of our group were horrified when they saw my wheelchair. Nahda hadn't told her in-laws. They couldn't imagine how it could go on the boat crossing.

More phone calls were made and eventually they took us to the house of an acquaintance, Uncle Ismael. It was about two o'clock in the afternoon, but I was so tired I just slept on the couch without saying a word to anyone.

When I woke up there were all these people we didn't know. I'm in big trouble now, I thought, because there will be all this investigation about why I am the way I am, how I was born early and all that. That's the part I hate when I meet people for the first time. I didn't say anything. I could have given a lecture about all the things I know. I could have told them how, because I couldn't develop properly physically, I replaced it with intellectual development and learnt new information every day. But that would have been awkward. Instead I just stared at the floor, so they probably thought I was autistic.

Then they started asking my sister why had we left with someone like me and how could we possibly make the long journey in a wheelchair. 'We had no choice,' said Nasrine.

The boat over to Greece was being organized by Uncle Ahmed, who had driven us from Manbij and would also be going with his wife Auntie Shereen. Our three cousins Mohammed, Dilba and Helda, whose parents had been killed in Kobane, were coming and Mohammed's wife Farmana, and

TOP LEFT Me and my brother Bland – he has been with me for every important event of my life.

TOP RIGHT At home in Manbij 2002 (aged three) in a special white dress Yaba (my father) bought me as a gift back from Mecca where he had gone on the Haj pilgrimage.

MIDDLE LEFT On the terrace of our apartment in Aleppo – my only interaction with the outside world.

MIDDLE RIGHT At Newroz 2009 – our traditional Kurdish new year celebrations – which was the only time I ever went out. We were made by the regime to go to a rocky place outside the city.

BOTTOM Yaba (my dad) and Ayee (my mum) in traditional Kurdish dress.

EPA

ABOVE AND LEFT Me and my mother on the edge of the Queiq river dam for a family picnic in 2009. The river flows through Aleppo and in 2013 was the scene of an awful massacre when 110 corpses appeared shot in the head.

LEFT Here I am at a family barbecue on the bank of the Euphrates river celebrating Newroz 2011, just before revolution then war swept the country.

BELOW After a series of operations in 2010.

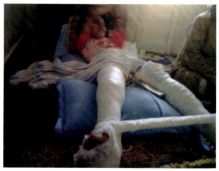

President Bashar al-Assad and his British-born wife Asma in 2003. When he took over in 2000 after the death of his father Hafez, we had great hopes but they soon faded.

Aleppo, with its ancient fortress in the background.

Much of the city has now been turned to rubble and hundreds of thousands of people have fled.

ABOVE Some of the biggest
demonstrations against
the regime in 2011 took
place in Hama after Friday
prayers in July and were
brutally put down; the
city had been the scene
of a crackdown by Hafez
al-Assad in 1987 which left
around 10,000 people dead.

LEFT Daesh militants moved
into Syria in 2014 and set up
their capital in Raqqa.

Arriving on the beach in
Lesbos after crossing in a
dinghy from Turkey on
2 September 2015.

Being taken away by Croatian police in a prison van – we were terrified we would be fingerprinted and forced to apply for asylum there.

BELOW Talking to BBC reporter Fergal Keane on our journey through Serbia – I told him I wanted to be an astronaut.

BELOW The Serbian-Hungarian border – we got there just as Hungary closed the fence and stopped letting people cross, leaving us stranded and forced to find another route.

In Germany at last, but waiting in a queue for five hours for a bus to a camp.
Nasrine's brithday, 21 September 2015.

Tired, bored and wanting to see my brother! In a refugee camp in the German city of Rosenheim.

RIGHT Almost at the end of our journey – the train to Cologne.

BELOW Reunited! Nasrine and I with Bland in our new home in Wesseling.

BELOW Meeting US ambassador to the United Nations Samantha Power in Berlin in June 2016.

BELOW The ancient city of Palmyra once ruled over by Queen Zenobia used to be a favourite tourist site. It was captured by Daesh in 2015 and many ancient buildings were destroyed, including the Arch of Triumph which had stood for eighteen hundred years.

VALERY SHARIFULIN\TASS VIA GETTY IMAGES

At Cologne Zoo, looking at the animals I knew about from the documentaries I used to watch all day and night in Aleppo.

Playing wheelchair basketball in my new chair in Germany, June 2016.

Exiled from their country; my brother Mustafa and my parents in Gaziantep, April 2016. I miss them terribly.

some other cousins and their children. In total we would be nineteen adults and eleven children – I guess at sixteen I could still be a child.

We'd thought we would only be in İzmir a short time, but the trip was obviously going to take us longer to arrange than we had imagined. I was glad when we moved again to a hotel even though it would use some of our precious cash. It was the Hotel Daria, which means sea in Kurdish, and Nasrine and I were in room 206, which is the number of bones in the human body.

The hotel was round the corner from Basmane Square and we went there each day. Everyone seemed to be on the phone haggling. It was kind of like an open-air travel agency with refugees negotiating passages with smugglers or their agents. I was shocked that some of the smugglers were Syrian, mostly from a town called Azaz which is notorious. Anyone who wasn't dealing in boats seemed to be buying or selling life jackets. Apart from the piles on the square, all the shops in the area, even the shoe shop and kebab shop, were selling them. Clothes shops displayed them on their mannequins over dresses as if they were fashion items.

Uncle Ahmed took us for lunch upstairs in Café Sinbad, which was the main place for swapping information and arranging passages. My cousin Mohammed carried me, which raised some eyebrows as I am past puberty. We had flatbread and kebabs, but most people were just smoking and drinking tea, trying to save their money.

131

On the TV was Angela Merkel, the Chancellor of Germany, which was where almost everyone was trying to get to as they had good benefits for migrants. There or Denmark or Sweden. There was good news. Early that morning, Merkel's government had tweeted that Syrians would no longer be subject to the Dublin regulation, so they would accept us in Germany even if we had been fingerprinted somewhere else.

Funny, after all the war documentaries I'd watched I had always thought of the Germans as the bad guys, and now they were our saviours. Maybe Mrs Merkel was trying to make amends for the past and Hitler, or maybe she was different because she grew up in East Germany behind the Berlin Wall which was built when she was seven.

Everyone in the café was trying to arrange passage to Greece. Some like us had come by road and plane, others by road the whole way. Many said they had sold all they had to come here, including heirlooms and family homes, or had borrowed money. One man said he had even met someone who had sold his kidney to fund the trip.

Some had already tried the crossing. We met one family who had failed because their dinghy was too overloaded and quickly sank. But they were trying again. 'Either you die from shelling in Syria or you die at sea,' shrugged the father. Though the Aegean crossing was much shorter and nowhere near as dangerous as the open sea between Libya and Lampedusa, at least fifty people had drowned making the crossing so far that year. 'There's no life left in Syria,' agreed someone else. 'It's like being in a burning house – it's risky to jump out of the window, but what's the alternative?'

The price was usually about $1,000 a person, but some people said it was better to get a wooden boat which was more expensive. We were trying to get some kind of motor-ised yacht because of my wheelchair, which everyone thought would be too heavy for a dinghy, so I'm always the obstacle. Mustafa's cousin Mahmud even said I shouldn't bring it.

While Uncle Ahmed was getting recommendations for smugglers, the rest of us went to buy life jackets. A good one cost 50 euros. People in the café had warned us not to buy the cheaper locally made ones which cost only 15 euros but were stuffed with foam or packaging which absorbs water and wouldn't float. Nahda's children were excited trying them on, except for one who cried. On the advice of the people in the café we also bought a pack of party balloons. They'd told us that the best way to protect the all-precious phone on the boat crossing was putting it inside a balloon.

As we went back to the hotel we crossed the square where people were speaking urgently on phones. 'You've got to decide now, spaces are running out!' we heard one man say. 'I've never lost a passenger,' insisted another.

Every evening around dusk, lines would gather on the square as tour buses arrived to collect those off to make the crossing as if they were going on holiday.

* * *

As if it wasn't bad enough that we needed a special boat because my wheelchair would weigh down the dinghy, Nasrine and I were delaying everyone because Shiar was supposed to be transferring the money for our passage and it didn't come. I knew that Mahmud and some of the others were saying they should go on without us. Eventually the money came through, and Uncle Ahmed called to say he had found a suitable boat and we would go the next night. I couldn't believe we were finally going. We didn't have much to get ready, but Nasrine rearranged our backpack to have something to do and charged the phone.

The next day the phone didn't ring. We kept checking it was on even though we knew it was. Then my uncle called. He told Nasrine that the smuggler had stopped answering his phone. We stayed up late, thinking at any moment the call would come, but nothing. When even at 2 a.m. he didn't answer, we knew this was a bad sign.

After two days we realized the man had disappeared and like a lot of people we had been cheated. Uncle Ahmed had paid a deposit, fortunately not too much.

Then the same thing happened again. We waited and waited because those proper boats were hard to find. As August came to an end we began to get worried. We heard that the sea was going mad, the waves getting higher and the water cold, and we were in a panic. The longer we waited the more dangerous it would be. We knew the others felt we were delaying them. In the end Uncle Ahmed said we would have to go in a dinghy but we would pay more to try to get one just for our family. It was decided that if the wheelchair became a problem in the boat we would get rid of it. No one said what would happen to me.

This time my uncle did it differently. To try and get round the cheating, a system had developed where you pay the money to a third party, then the money is only released to the smuggler once you are safely across. The way it works is you pay the money to an 'insurance office' and they give you a numeric code. Then once you reach Greece you call and give the code to the agent so he can collect the money. If a passenger doesn't call after three days, the smuggler can also get the money, so they get paid even if the person drowns.

Compared to some people's experiences, we were lucky. We met a family with a toddler and a ten-day-old baby girl sleeping outside on the front terrace of the mosque because they had lost everything. They told us they were from Deraa where the revolution had started and they had fled after their house was destroyed in a bombing raid. They had left so hurriedly that the woman Rasha gave birth along the way. It had taken them twenty days to get to İzmir, then they had paid a smuggler $2,700 for the crossing and he had disappeared.

Like I told you when I talked about the Nujeen principles, I don't like to believe that people are evil by nature, but when I met people like the people smugglers I wasn't sure I was right. They were taking the money of people who had already lost almost everything and were leaving them begging. Then there were ones who sent people, even children, to sea in substandard boats. I don't like to judge someone, but what kind of man sends someone to die and makes money from it?

It made me remember the discussion Nasrine and I had had back in Aleppo in 2006, when Saddam Hussein was executed. I was confused because I felt sorry. I mean, we all know what Saddam did to the Kurds – this was personal for us. But Nasrine told me there's no shame in feeling sorry, what we wanted was justice not revenge, and anyway he shouldn't have been executed on the Eid holiday.

The Ramadan before we left Turkey, there was a TV programme about verses of the Koran and how they came to the Prophet (Peace Be Upon Him). One of them was the story of the Ethiopian man who murdered the Prophet's uncle Hamza the Brave with a spear. The Prophet forgave him, and the man became a Muslim and later used the same spear to slay a false Prophet. I was so happy that the Koran supported my view of the ultimate good nature of people.

But the people smugglers really tested that. And they were making so much money. I calculated that if on average people were paying $1,000 each and the smuggler squashed in as many as sixty then that's $60,000 each crossing. Even after you take away the cost of the boat and commissions to agents and the bus to the beach, they must make at least $30,000 per crossing. So far that year 300,000 people had crossed that way – that's millions of dollars!

In Café Sinbad, we watched the news on CNN and Al Arabiya. Most reports seemed to be about the 'Refugee Crisis', showing crowds of people arriving on the Greek islands and in Macedonia, Hungary and Austria, exactly where we were going.

On 31 August we saw Mrs Merkel again giving a press conference, calling on the EU to do better. 'If Europe fails on the question of refugees, then it won't be the Europe we wished for,' she said. 'We live in orderly, very orderly circumstances,' she added. 'Most of us do not know the feeling of complete exhaustion combined with fear.' She ended by saying, *'Wir schaffen das'* – 'We can do this.' I like that woman. Maybe she will be our Queen Zenobia.

Finally, the day after that, on our tenth day in İzmir, the call came. Uncle Ahmed had found a boat to take us to Lesbos. It was our turn to go.

11

The Route of Death

Behram to Lesbos, Wednesday 2 September 2015

It was after midnight when the bus finally picked us up from Basmane Square where we had all been waiting for hours with our life jackets and few belongings. Other waiting groups had gone and each time we were left behind. Finally, ours came. My cousin Mohammed carried me on and I told Nasrine to make sure the wheelchair didn't get left behind by those who were against our bringing it. Then we drove through the night, most of us dropping off to sleep.

Suddenly the bus screeched to a stop. The doors opened and Turkish gendarmerie got in, flashing their torches like one of those old war movies of Nazis searching for Jews. What could we say? We told them the truth, that we were Syrians fleeing war. They told us we must go back to where we came from. The bus turned round and started heading towards İzmir. I couldn't believe we were going to return after all that. But the driver was a nice man. After a couple of miles he pulled over and told us to get out and wait for a bit and someone else would come and get us. It was about 5 a.m. The place where he had dropped us was an abandoned olive-oil factory. We huddled by the walls, shivering in the pre-dawn darkness, away from the pools of light thrown by the street-lamps, worried about being spotted again by the gendarmerie. I saw that Nahda was weeping. One of her little girls had got left behind on the bus. Luckily the driver noticed and brought her back within a few minutes.

As soon as the sun rose my uncle kept calling the smuggler, but he was not answering. 'Not again!' I said. The glare of the sun was becoming unbearable, and I feared we were in an endless vicious circle of being conned.

Finally the smuggler answered, and after nine hours, at around 2 p.m., five taxis came to pick us all up. They drove us along the main road overlooking the sea, past the turn-off to Assos, and pulled into the side of the road by an olive grove.

'Wow,' I exclaimed as I was lifted out into my chair. Inside the taxi we had been too crowded to really see out, but now we could see green fields dotted with grey rocks and gnarled olive trees leading down to a sparkling blue sea. I gazed about in wonder. Just west of us on a cliff were what must have been the ancient columns of Assos and the ruins of Aristotle's school of philosophers. Across the water was a dark rocky island. 'That's it, Greece,' said Uncle Ahmed.

The Route of Death

Nasrine punched into her phone the Google coordinates we had been given for our departure point and we began the walk down to the shore. Google said 1.1 miles, which wasn't far, but we couldn't use the road that wound down in case we were spotted and instead had to walk through the olive groves. The way down was hard and rocky and Nasrine and one of my cousins had to carry me in my chair much of the way as it was impossible for the wheels. Soon my back was hurting badly as we were bumping around and I was jolting so much, but everyone kept saying, 'You are the Queen, Queen Nujeen in your chair.' I felt like one of those ancient monarchs being carried in a litter like I'd seen King Herod in a biopic of Joseph, who we call Yusuf.

When we got to the shore, it wasn't sandy as I had imagined it would be, so my chair still couldn't move. We thought we were in the right place as there were discarded nappies, clothes and medicines all over the beach and old life jackets, evidence everywhere of refugees.

But it turned out that somehow we were at the point used by another smuggler. The right place was half a mile further along the shore, but there was a cliff in the way and no way round. The only way there was to climb the hill and then go down. It was hard enough getting up but coming back down with my wheelchair was almost impossible as it was slippery and rocks kept being dislodged. Everyone was getting very hot and bothered. There was a group of people down below already waiting who could see we were struggling, so six

Moroccan guys came up to help. Somehow they had rope with them which they used to tie the wheelchair and make a kind of pulley system.

Finally, we made it. By then it was five in the afternoon and the sea was sparkling in the lowering sun. This beach was also littered with refugee debris, but we didn't care. We were tired and happy to be there. Some boats were going out, but they told us ours would not go till the morning and we would have to sleep in the olive grove. So it was another cold night outside. I'd never heard waves lapping on a shore before, and I listened to them and the breeze in the trees until they lulled me to sleep.

The smuggler, who was Turkish but a Kurd so we'd trusted him, arrived next morning with the boats in 'Made in China' boxes for us and the other groups waiting. When our dinghy was inflated Uncle Ahmed became very angry. We had paid extra to have a new dinghy, but it was clear this was an old one and there was a big repair patch on the bottom. Also the outboard motor was only 20 horsepower instead of the usual 30. The smuggler just shrugged. What could we do? We couldn't go back to İzmir and start the whole process again.

By 11a.m. all four boats were prepared and we were all ready in our life jackets, but the smuggler said he was waiting for the Turkish coastguards out at sea to move away.

Then it was all day waiting with nothing to drink, no food but sugar cubes and Nutella, and nothing to do but stare at the water we had to cross. We got tired and took the life jackets off. In the afternoon the wind began getting up and the waves got higher. I started to think we were going to die on the beach. Around 4.30 p.m. the smuggler told us to put our life jackets back on and each group to have their driver ready. In our case this was Uncle Ahmed, but the other groups didn't seem to have realized they would have no pilot and hadn't chosen. Then at 5 p.m. the coastguard shift changed and it was time to go. Nadha and her husband Mustafa bid each other goodbye as he was staying behind to look after his parents.

The motors were attached and the dinghies pushed into the water, then everyone waded through the shallows to clamber in, some of them carrying small children in their arms. Suddenly I realized I was the only one left on the shore. In her anxiety to go even Nasrine had climbed on board. 'What about me?' I yelled.

Our Moroccan friends were still waiting for their boat, so they carried me out to the dinghy in the chair and lifted me in.

'Goodbye, Turkey,' I said as Uncle Ahmed started the engine.

*   *   *

From the sea the island looked much further away. Our dark grey dinghy was very small. Even though we had paid extra just to be the thirty-eight of us, which was much better than the fifty or so we had seen crammed into earlier boats, it was still more than double the '15 Max' it said on the box, particularly with my wheelchair, and it felt very squashed.

Like everything I was doing, it was my first time on a boat. I felt like a six-year-old girl not a sixteen-year-old. 'Why are you nervous?' asked Nasrine. 'I am not nervous, I'm excited doing everything for the first time,' I replied. 'It's not excitement, it's fear,' she said. 'Don't be afraid.' She never showed her own fear because she knew everything she did would affect me. She was the one who knew the outside world and I took all my cues on how to react from her.

I did my deep breathing from *Brain Games* and looked around the boat at everyone. We were all spaced out from two days with little sleep, then being in the hot sun with nothing to drink. My three cousins whose mother and father had been shot were sad and quiet. Many people had closed their eyes and were praying. Nasrine was crouching on the floor trying to hold my chair still.

Our elder sister Nahda didn't look at the sea. Her baby and the three little girls were all crying and she was focused on calming them. She was stressed because she'd decided to take her children out of the poisoned environment of war to somewhere they could get on with life, go to school, but now it seemed like a big responsibility for a thirty-three-year-old alone and she wondered what she had done.

Uncle Ahmed was all furrow-browed trying to drive the boat. He'd spent the last two days in the hotel in İzmir studying YouTube videos on how to do it. At the start he gunned the engine too much and we shot forward then zigzagged a bit as he tried to correct the course. 'Look out!' shouted Aunt Shereen as we bumped right into a wave and water came over the sides. The sea was much less calm than it had looked earlier in the day. To start with it was nice to feel the spray after being in the hot sun all day. Finally, my 'Young Forever Love' T-shirt I had worn for days was getting a wash. But as waves pitched us up and down, some of my cousins started retching. Others were crying and screaming 'Oh God!'

At one point a wave tossed us right to one side and my aunt lost her bag with all her valuables. We seemed very low in the water. My cousins used their shoes to scoop water out of the dinghy. Sometimes people throw things off but we didn't have much. 'We should never have brought the wheelchair,' said Mahmud.

I felt I should be worried – I knew this water might be our grave. And of course I can't swim. I'd never been in water. None of us could swim. Yet sitting in my wheelchair, higher than everyone else, I thought of myself like Poseidon, God of the Sea, in his chariot. I tried to imagine the hippocampus, the half-horse half-fish that towed it along, and fancied that through the spray of mist I could see the Nereides, the daughters of Poseidon, riding the horse fish, tossing their long hair and laughing in the wind.

I smiled at the thought. 'Look, Nahda, how beautiful it is!' I cried as we were tossed up and down. I laughed every time we were hit by another wave even though we were drenched through. 'You need a psychiatrist, laughing here,' said someone. Actually I was praying too, but quietly.

We were so intent on our own boat that we didn't see what happened to the other three leaving with us. But Mustafa, scrambling up the cliff to follow our journey with binoculars and report back to our parents, was horrified. As he watched, the first boat left with the waves and was quickly overturned. We were the second boat to go. The third got much of the way and overturned close to the island, leaving the people to swim. The fourth was picked up by the Turkish coastguard. Mustafa was in tears on the phone to my father because he didn't know if it was us. In fact we were better off as there were fewer of us compared with the other boats and Uncle Ahmed's YouTube lessons had proved useful. He went against the waves instead of with them and got us to sit more on the side where the waves were hitting the boat to keep it down.

After a while a mist came down and we could no longer see Lesbos ahead. I hoped we were going the right way. Mahmud kept looking at my wheelchair. I knew we had agreed that if it became a danger we would throw it into the sea, but surely he wouldn't really do that.

I kept an eye out for pirates and Turkish coastguards, but the only people at sea seemed to be refugees. Hundreds of people were making the crossing every day and two other dinghies were not far behind us. I didn't realize how close death was. Just a small tear in the fabric from my wheelchair catching and we could have capsized or a large wave could have turned the boat over at any moment.

That's what happened to another Syrian family making the crossing the same day. We didn't know then but crossing earlier that day in those choppy waters a little south of us from the Bodrum peninsula to Kos was a dinghy like ours. Inside were sixteen Syrians including a barber called Abdullah Kurdi, his wife Rehanna and their two little boys, five-year-old Ghalib and three-year-old Aylan. Like us they were Kurds from Kobane and were hoping to start a new life in Germany.

Though the crossing to Kos is short, just 4 miles, even shorter than the 8 miles from Behram to Lesbos, the sea further south is more exposed and after an hour bouncing on the waves, a larger one came and flipped the dinghy with no warning, tossing everyone out. Abdullah tried to cling on to his little family but one after the other they were washed away. He stayed three hours in the water desperately searching but they were lost. Eleven of the passengers drowned, five of them children.

The next day the photograph of little Aylan Kurdi lying face down dead in the surf on a Turkish beach, in his smart red shirt and long blue shorts, went round the world. When I saw it later on Facebook, I thought that could have been me. I had to turn the phone off and take a deep breath and try and think to myself, He's an innocent boy, he's in heaven and happy now.

When I discussed it with my sisters we all agreed: if we had heard about it before our crossing, we would have gone back to Gaziantep.

For a normal person, the ferry from western Turkey to Mitilini, the capital of Lesbos, costs 10 euros and takes ninety minutes. To make the same crossing as refugees had taken us twelve days to arrange and cost us each $1,500.

We had been at sea three and a half hours and the sun was setting and we were starting to shiver when suddenly there was the island rising like a giant black rock ahead of us. Soon we could make out people waiting on the shore. 'Does anybody speak English?' we heard someone shout. 'I do!' I called out. Everyone looked at me. That was a turning point in my life, even more than when Nasrine had said it was all right to feel sorry for Saddam being executed. It was the first time I had spoken English to a real English-speaker.

12

Freedom like a Normal Person

Lesbos, 2 September–9 September 2015

It felt as if we had taken a salty shower. The dinghy bumped on to the rocky shore and friendly faces and outstretched hands awaited us with towels, bottles of water and biscuits. Some of my relatives were too dazed to get out on their own and volunteers walked into the sea and helped us. They were surprised to see my wheelchair and lifted it out on to the shore. 'You are the first refugee we have seen in a wheelchair,' they told me.

My aunt Shereen kissed the shore and started praying. Others hugged each other or the volunteers. Nahda was crying. Some just started walking up the beach. One of my cousins remembered to take a knife to puncture the dinghy because the smuggler had told us that if it was still seaworthy the Greek coastguards might send us back. A fisherman came and took the motor.

The person who had asked if anyone spoke English was a Spanish photo-journalist. He asked me how the trip had been.

'I enjoyed it because I don't think I will have the chance again,' I said.

'Is it the first time you have seen the sea?' he asked.

'Yes, and it looks beautiful for me,' I smiled.

'What do you expect from Europe?' was his last question.

I thought for a moment as this was important. 'I expect freedom like a normal person,' I replied.

We had landed in a place called Skala Sikamineas, a little fishing village on the northern shore of Lesbos where many of the boats arrived. We knew Greece was in economic trouble so we were overwhelmed by how kind people were. Among the volunteers on the beach were three old women in black who brought warm milk for Nahda's baby and reminded me of my grandmother in Kobane. We found out later that like many on Lesbos their own mothers and fathers had come to the island on boats as refugees from İzmir when it was called Smyrna, at the time that it was a mostly Greek city. Turkish soldiers attacked it in 1922 during the Greco-Turkish war, slaughtering Greeks and setting fire to the historic centre. Thousands fled across the Aegean Sea.

The old ladies led us along the shore to a little harbour of brightly painted fishing boats with a tiny white church on a rock called Our Lady of the Mermaid, and people sitting at tables outside bars eating and drinking. The village was so beautiful it looked like a postcard. Across the way was a community centre where there was a room full of dry clothes donated by local people. We pulled off the wet clothes stiff with salt and put on new ones. Nothing quite fitted and we laughed at the kids in adult-sized shirts with arms flapping.

The volunteers explained that there would be a bus next morning to the main town and port of Mitilini where refugees had to get registered in order to travel onwards. In the meantime we would have to spend the night outdoors up on the main road where the bus would stop because there was nowhere to sleep. My English was proving very useful. It was like I was official translator for the group. For the first time in my life everyone needed me!

Then someone came in talking fast in Greek. They told us that there had been a tragedy and a dinghy after us had overturned. 'The Moroccans!' I gasped. I was heartbroken.

It was getting dark and before we did anything else we needed to eat as we were starving. We went to a café by a large mulberry tree and I ordered a sandwich. It looked so weird to me and also tasted odd. I had expected all Western food to be beautifully presented like I had seen on *Masterchef*. 'What is this?' I asked the waitress. 'Don't worry, it's not pig,' she replied, 'it's turkey.' Anyway it tasted horrible. Western food always tastes raw to me, as our Kurdish food is much more cooked.

As always Nasrine complained about me being fussy but went to find a grocers to buy some biscuits. When she came back she said she had met a Syrian who told her that he and his family had first tried to cross through Bulgaria like Bland only to get stuck in the forest for ten days. Eventually they ran out of water and came out of the forest, so police had arrested them and sent them back to Turkey. They then decided to cross the sea to Greece, but 2 miles from shore their dinghy had capsized and they'd had to swim. We realized how lucky we had been.

The way up through the village to the road was extremely steep and it was going to be very hard to push me. But local authorities had made it illegal for private citizens to drive refugees. There was a Turkish aid-worker called Sardar eating at the next table in the restaurant and he overheard us. 'She can't walk up there!' he said. He went to the police and got special permission to drive me. He drove me and Nasrine, but the rest of the group had to walk the couple of miles up through the village. Disability benefits again!

Sadly, even those only went so far. Sardar left us by the roadside where he said the bus would come and gave me his phone number. There was a kind of parking lot where other refugees were sleeping. Our third night in the open and this one was the worst of all because we were right at the foot of a sheer cliff. It was a terrible night. I remembered Road

Runner cartoons and thought a large rock from the cliff would fall and crush me. I tried to sleep in my wheelchair but couldn't. I was stiff and bruised from the bumping through the olive groves and then in the boat.

Eventually dawn broke and the sun came out all at once like a big pale grapefruit. Someone shouted out 'Nujeen!' To our delight it was the Moroccan guys who had helped us. They told us their dinghy had indeed overturned but they could swim, so they had still made it. I was so relieved.

We waited and waited for the bus to come but there was no sign of it. It got hotter and hotter and other people started walking, but Lesbos is a big island and it was more than 30 miles to the refugee camp near the port. Nasrine said she would push me, but I thought it would take days and we would melt in the 39°C heat.

Fortunately, my phone was still picking up the Turkish service so I called Sardar and told him we were stranded. He arranged for a young local woman volunteer called Kristine to come and collect me and Nasrine. She arrived about midday in a small yellow car crammed with provisions for refugees like water and biscuits. It was so full it was hard to get in. There was no way Nahda and her children could fit in so Kristine told her to wait and she would come back for her. The rest of the family had already left on foot.

It was a long twisty drive of an hour but simply beautiful. We followed a winding road along the sea, passing what seemed an endless line of refugees walking. The sea was on one side and the other side were forests of gnarled olive trees and beyond them mountains. Kristine told us that the island was famous for olives. That made me think of Uncle Bozan and I was sad. We passed an old Byzantine castle on the waterfront and started to see the outskirts of a town with stone houses and tiled roofs – Mitilini. Kristine left us at a café and I ordered a hot chocolate in English. We waited there for two hours while she went back to pick up Nahda and her children.

While we waited we watched tourists with their boiled-lobster skins, oversized sunglasses and straw hats, smelling of coconut oil and ordering colourful cocktails. I thought how deceptive this is, people are enjoying their holidays and no one knows that just down there are families sleeping on the road who have fled war and bombings.

The main refugee camp in Lesbos is called Moria. We were shocked when we saw it. It was a former military base and looked like a prison with high walls and barbed wire. And there were so many people. A camp official wrote numbers on our wrists with marker pens and took us to a hut crowded with other refugees. The place was filthy and many people seemed to be ill, coughing or suffering from stomach problems. When we saw the bathroom and toilet it was not appropriate for me – there was nothing for a disabled person to hold on to.

The rest of our party were still walking along the road towards the camp, but we couldn't see how we could stay in such a place. So Kristine took us to another camp near the shore called Pikpa which had been set up by a charity for the sick or those more in need. It was meant to be for Syrian families but there were Afghans and Iraqis. Pikpa had wooden bungalows but those were all full, so volunteers led us to a family ridge tent 12 foot by 12 foot. There were me, my two sisters and four nieces and also Mohammed, Mustafa's nephew, who was supposed to look after Nahda.

Next to us was another Syrian family with a young girl whose eyes were very red and infected. They told us their dinghy had capsized because the engine failed and they were eleven hours in the water before being rescued. Another family told us that so much water had come into their dinghy they had thrown everything out, even the bag with their gold jewellery and money, so they had been left with nothing.

We were given mats to sleep on but some people were sleeping on cardboard. The camp was near the airport and there was a barrage of noise from the planes coming low overhead and from all the children. It reminded me of Manbij and the bombing and I covered my ears. I hated it there. The place was too hot in the day and full of mosquitoes at night. Nahda's children kept whining and my sisters kept moaning about the lack of hygiene – there was rubbish everywhere and other refugees referred to it as the Jungle. There were separate toilets for men and women, but not bathrooms. Only a curtain separated men from women and it smelt so disgusting no one could endure it for more than five minutes. I noticed a lot of the women were veiled and complaining that it was not possible for them to do the ablutions we do before prayers. Some of the men bathed in the sea. Nasrine and Nahda wanted to wash our clothes but there was a long queue to use the sink.

Everyone we met stared at my wheelchair and asked, 'Oh! How did she get here?' One of the volunteers told me she had seen me on TV. That interview I had given on arriving had made me famous! It's funny because I always forget I am in a wheelchair. Whenever I imagine myself in a tourist attraction like the Victoria and Albert Museum in London, I picture myself walking. I forget I will be in a wheelchair with someone pushing me.

Bland had told us that the first thing we should do each time we got to a new country was get a local SIM card. We found people selling them, bottles of water and top-up cards at the gate, and there was a charging area in the camp which you had to queue for – everyone wanted to charge their phone. There were coloured pencils for children and some of their drawings had been pinned up. Some were of houses with stick-figure families at the door and bomber planes overhead. One of them showed a flower dripping blood.

It was while waiting there for our phones to charge that we first heard about little Aylan Kurdi. I refused to look at the photograph as I knew it would be bad for my psychology.

* * *

Freedom like a Normal Person

It was a tough week that we spent in Lesbos. The Greeks were going through their own crisis. The country was bankrupt and half their young people couldn't find jobs. The last thing they needed was us refugees. Not surprisingly there was little to eat in the camp. They gave out spaghetti but we had nothing to cook it on. Every day my sisters bought tomatos and a kind of salami made of beef, and some bread to make sandwiches. After a week I said I am not going to eat salami again for another year. Nasrine complained that the Greeks were keeping us refugees there deliberately to make money for their economy.

But the volunteers were very friendly. And they were just overwhelmed by the numbers. Soon there would be 37,000 refugees on the island, almost half its population. Mohammed went into the town to investigate ferry times and tickets, and said he saw lots of people sleeping in parks and on the streets.

My English was proving useful and I was glad because I felt I had had to learn it in a very hard way with no books or lessons. One day a volunteer asked me to translate for a Kurdish lady whose daughter was sick. She had a kidney infection and they wanted me to explain about the medicine. Afterwards the woman couldn't stop thanking me. 'I am so happy, you are my angel,' she said. All because of *Days of Our Lives!*

* * *

Even though we were all trying to escape from fighting, I guess so many desperate people crowded together and wanting to be somewhere else is bound to cause tension and fights broke out. To travel on from Lesbos to the mainland you needed a paper from the Greek government granting permission to stay three weeks. The Greeks had set up a fast-track system for Syrians to be processed in just two days, while other nationalities could take more than a month. This of course annoyed the others, particularly Afghans and Iraqis who were also fleeing from war. One day there was a commotion. A big fight had broken out and Afghans and Iraqis had set fire to the centre containing all the paperwork in protest against the special treatment for Syrians.

This slowed everything for everyone. Nahda was getting really annoyed, worried that her children would get sick in the heat and dirt, and she kept asking me to talk to people and to call Sardar and Kristine. Finally, on the seventh day, we were told that police were coming and we should gather in the central square. Eventually Greek officials came and took our names, dates of birth and where we came from. People were scared to give fingerprints because of that Dublin regulation even though the Germans had said it didn't matter.

When it came to our turn I was the translator. I explained we were Kurds fleeing Aleppo and had no papers. It was hard to concentrate as the policeman had a cup of coffee on his table which I couldn't stop looking at because I wanted to drink it so much.

Freedom like a Normal Person

By the end of that day we had the precious permission. It said Greek authorities wouldn't exercise their right to arrest us and was valid for three weeks. The piece of paper felt like one of Willy Wonka's golden tickets. There was no point in staying any longer. There was a ferry that night that in twelve hours would take us to Athens for 60 euros each. But we ended up staying another night as Mohammed forgot to take our permissions when he went to buy the tickets. So the rest of our relatives, who were all in Moria, ended up going on without us.

The next evening we called a taxi for eight o'clock, before sunset, but it did not come. We waited at the front of the camp. The guard had six dogs so I went mad as they were all around. Finally at midnight the taxi came and drove us to the port. We got out in front of a beautiful old building like rich people in Europe owned centuries ago and I wondered who had lived there.

The ferry to Athens was going at 3 a.m. and the terminal was full of other refugees waiting. Some people had put up small tents and were sleeping. Nahda and her kids huddled together on the steps of the customs building. Just as I was about to doze off in my chair, once again a swarm of dogs appeared, maybe twelve or thirteen of them, all snapping around. I couldn't believe it. It's like these wild animals follow me.

Nasrine tried to quieten me. 'Calm down,' she said. 'Look, there's a beautiful puppy.'

'It's not a beautiful puppy, it's a monster!' I snarled.

Then we saw the ferry gliding in with shiny green lights. It was so big, like a multi-storey building, I couldn't imagine how it would enter the port. I thought we would have to go to it on a small boat, but it came right on against the pier.

Finally at 4 a.m. the police told us we could board. They took me to the front of the queue, so I was the first one on. The ferry had five decks – our seats were on the third deck and for once there was a lift up.

I could hear the hum of the engine, then we felt the ferry moving. Nasrine went up to the top deck to watch the sun rise over the terracotta roofs of Mitilini as we sailed away.

I was excited. It was my first time on a ship. And we were going to the birthplace of democracy. But I was exhausted. We weren't even out of the port when I fell asleep.

13

Through the Beautiful Gate

Athens to Macedonia, 10–15 September 2015

I stared fixedly at the angel on the wall of the hotel room as if I could make it fly. Maybe it sounds crazy, but more than anything I wanted to do the journey like everybody else.

The rest of our relatives had all headed north to the border with Macedonia, fearful that the police would close it because there were so many thousands of refugees massing there. Uncle Ahmed, Aunt Shereen and all our cousins had set off even before we got to Athens.

Nahda's in-laws had waited for us to arrive on the ferry, the day before. I was excited to land in Athens but the port of Piraeus was huge and confusing and so reeked of fish it made my throat gag. As Nasrine pushed me down the ramp, we saw a miserable encampment of refugees in makeshift tents on the dockside. We could also hear shouting – a group of port workers protesting against it being sold off. Then, like blood-sucking flies, the smugglers appeared, asking, 'Want to fly, go by land, need a passport?' We tried to get a taxi but they were charging triple what we had been told to pay. Luckily one of Nahda's in-laws took us to catch a train, which was a bit complicated to navigate with the wheelchair but much cheaper. Sometimes it feels as if everyone is trying to cheat refugees.

Nahda's in-laws were staying in an apartment in Athens with greasy walls and no windows arranged for them by the smuggler they had paid to get them to Macedonia. They cooked us eggs and tomatoes while Mohammed went to find us a hotel room near by as they would be leaving the next morning, catching a bus at ten o'clock to take them to the Macedonian border. It's not so easy booking hotels as refugees. Often they turn us away or charge more because we don't have papers. It's like they think we are dirty or criminals – we are just the same as everyone else but we have lost our homes. Where we were staying was called the New Dream Hotel. Our room had blue lights and a painting of an angel over the bed. Nahda stayed with her relatives as she would be leaving with them. They bought us some bread and halal salami, and we hugged Nahda goodbye and wished each other luck.

* * *

So it was just me and Nasrine, the two sisters, if not the three musketeers. It was the first time we had ever had to fend for ourselves on our own, let alone in a big foreign city. I turned on the TV, an old black and white one, and clicked through the channels with the remote looking for something in English. Finally I found one – an MTV show called *I Used to Be Fat*. I lay on the bed and was transported back to the old days of being on the fifth floor in Aleppo.

From the bathroom I heard water running and singing. 'Hot water!' shouted Nasrine. 'It's so nice to be clean!' It was the first time in the eleven days since we had left İzmir that we could properly wash. All we needed now were clean clothes. We were still using the ones we had got when we landed on Lesbos.

Our family hadn't just abandoned us to our fate. Shiar was flying in and the plan was for him to arrange fake passports for us which were supposed to be easy to get in Athens, and use those to buy a plane ticket straight to Germany so that we wouldn't have to do the overland journey. Everyone thought such a journey was too arduous to do in a wheelchair. Maybe they thought we would slow them down.

I was sad. 'Do you know what, Nasrine?' I said. 'I want to do it like everyone else. Do you know what that means?'

'Yes, I do too,' she replied.

Soon Shiar arrived, as usual full of talk. He told us to stay in the room and keep the curtains closed. This was very annoying as I was desperate to see the Acropolis. I couldn't believe we were in this ancient city, this birthplace of democracy and philosophy and Aristotle, and we would just hide behind curtains. But Nasrine said we shouldn't go out. There had been attacks on refugees from members of a party called Golden Dawn which might sound innocuous but they are ultra-right and have kind of swastikas on their flags.

We kept hearing sirens. Athens looked wealthy to us with its coffee shops and trendy bars, but we had noticed lots of homeless people. The debt crisis had left half its young people unemployed and those who could were leaving the country. Greece was in such bad shape it had had to be bailed out twice by international institutions and had just had a third bail-out with tough conditions imposed by the Germans. Banks were closed. There were daily protests in Syntagma Square in front of the parliament with police using teargas to disperse the crowds. I watched all this on TV in between some of my old favourite programmes. I was trying to overcome my aversion to watching news as we needed to know what was happening on the migrant trail.

Only once did Shiar and Nasrine take me out. Of course they didn't take me to the Parthenon, just to a Turkish restaurant for a kebab. The city looked so old and more Eastern to me than Western. We noticed a lot of old men playing with dice. On the menu, the Greek alphabet seemed strange to me, like Hebrew. It was dark when we came out of the restaurant, but there were people everywhere. It was the first time I'd seen a city so alive at night, but it reminded me of Aleppo. I tried not to think about what was happening there. I know Nasrine looked on Facebook.

Every day while Shiar went to Victoria Square to deal with smugglers, Nasrine and I studied maps of Europe on our phone and checked Facebook groups for migrants such as 'The Safe and Free Route to Asylum for Syrians' which gave tips on what refugees need and advice about the best routes. In between I kept staring at the angel and begging please, please, let me do it in the normal way.

Sometimes God answers your prayers. After a few days, Shiar told us it was proving very hard and too expensive to arrange the passports and he didn't know what to do.

Nasrine and I looked at each other. 'You know what,' she said. 'What if we just go by land?'

Yes! From a total jail to total freedom. I knew this would be a once-in-a-lifetime experience for me. I thought, I will have something to tell my grandchildren, just as my parents talk about 1973 when we had the war against Israel – they used to say that was a bad year, the year of the war. It would be hard for Nasrine pushing me but lots of fun.

And for once I would be like everyone else.

*　*　*

We took the 4.30 p.m. train from the main station to Thessaloniki, a six-hour journey. It was my first time on a train. Even though most refugees go to the border by bus as it is cheaper, the platform was crowded with other refugees, many of them with small children; there were also lots of tourists in shorts and T-shirts with big backpacks. When the train came, it was covered in graffiti. Everyone surged forward and I wondered how we would get on, but someone helped us and we found seats. All the seats looked worn. Someone told us that the Greek railway was losing so much money that if they gave all their passengers the taxi fare instead of running the trains it would have cost them less. I watched the scenery flash past – sun-baked fields, green mountains, black swallows slicing the sky, reddening sun – it was transfixing. The train was going so fast compared to everything outside it made me think about relativity theory. 'What would happen if the train goes at the speed of light?' I asked Nasrine. 'What would we see?' She said because of something called time dilation, the time will be fixed and you will get wherever you are going without witnessing any time passing for anything not moving with you. So the sun we could see as we sped by would always look red like the sunset. I didn't really understand, but I would do my research later. Then she said it wasn't possible to go at the speed of light, anyway. In other words she wanted me to shut up.

She went to fetch some drinks, and my imagination began running away with itself as it likes to do if I don't control it.

I couldn't stop thinking about movies where the train falls off the cliff. If that happened and I lost Nasrine, how would I get to the border on my own?

Fortunately, it didn't happen. It got dark outside and we tried to sleep. A rumour went round that Greek police were throwing refugees off as our papers didn't let us travel so far north. Some people locked themselves in the toilet, but no police came. Finally, it was our stop, Thessaloniki. The buses on to the border had stopped for the night, so people began negotiating with taxi drivers outside. 'We're not tourists,' we heard one man complain at the high prices. Some of them decided to spend the night at the station and find the bus the next morning, but we wanted to get on our way so we paid the 100 euros and took a taxi.

We knew from the Facebook groups that you couldn't cross the border at night, so our taxi driver drove us 55 miles to a town near the border called Evzonoi. There we checked into the Hara Hotel – the last hotel in Greece. Or the first, depending which way you are coming. A sign in the car park had a Greek man in white pantaloons holding out a red fez and saying, 'Welcome to Greece'.

The hotel was a kind of rundown place just off the motorway that had been about to close down until it was saved by the refugee crisis. Now people were coming and going non-stop. Some like us were staying, but the hotel had also turned its bar into a mini-market, selling refugee food like tinned sardines and biscuits as well as nappies and baby wipes. We were starving and went into the restaurant. The room had striplights like the hospitals I had been in and everything looked yellow. We ordered a pizza and it was the first time I had ever used a knife and fork. It was very awkward as it is *haram* for us Muslims to eat with our left hand so I was trying to use both the knife and the fork with my right.

In the distance we could see the lights of Macedonian casinos where Greeks go and gamble at night even though they don't really like Macedonia and think it should be theirs. That's why they claim Alexander the Great as Greek when he is really a Macedon. They don't even call it Macedonia but refer to it as FYROM – Former Yugoslav Republic of Macedonia. Even so they could just cross the border normally. We had to go through a field.

The next morning there was a WhatsApp message on Nasrine's phone from Nahda. 'Made it!' it said. They were already in Germany, having made the journey in just five days. 'See, how hard can it be?' I asked Nasrine.

Before we could set off on our journey we had to sort out a problem with my transport. There was a rubber band holding up the footrest of my wheelchair, but as we had come down the ramp at the ferry the band had snapped and the footrest had broken. This just left my feet dangling which was very uncomfortable. Luckily we found a nice man with a black hat and a pet bird who fixed wire round it for me to rest my feet on.

Nasrine pushed me along the main road. The sun was just coming up and everywhere was very green with forested hills all around. I'd never heard such a chatter of birds, but it was freezing cold. Ever since my asthma days I always feel the cold and am the first to get sick. Nasrine says I am a virus magnet. We weren't sure if we were going the right way, but then we came to a disused railway track like Nahda had described where crowds of people were waiting, held back by police clad in black like Ninjas. Other police watched on from vans on a ridge overlooking the tracks.

Evzonoi used to be a small town but now it was packed with thousands of refugees like us. A temporary transit centre had been set up and there were some Greek women handing out nappies and biscuits. Macedonian police with guns and truncheons made us get into groups of fifty to cross. We were put into one of three groups of what they call SIA – Syrians, Iraqis and Afghans – who were allowed to cross. Bangladeshis, Moroccans and so on had to go an illegal way. We had to walk about half a mile but the path was OK, though we were slower than everyone. The Greek police even helped us get my wheelchair over the railway line. There was nothing marking the border, just the black line on the GPS on our phone. Later we heard they put up a makeshift border point called Stone 59.

Once we were into Macedonia, the way was rocky and more difficult. The wheelchair kept getting stuck in the stones. Luckily some Macedonian guys selling biscuits saw our plight and helped. They turned my wheelchair back to front and pulled it.

There was a stream of people all heading the same way. Some were carrying babies on their backs or shoulders – Nahda must have done that a few days before. One man was limping, maybe wounded in a bombing raid. No one really spoke. Everyone looked desperate. I was the only one smiling. People were in a hurry because we had all heard that the Hungarians were starting to fence off their border so we needed to get there fast.

Eventually we came to a beautiful field of sunflowers, just as described on Facebook, with a well-trodden path through the middle. Either side was a mess of discarded water bottles and plastic bags and shoes and sleeping bags and other migrant litter, which was a bit sad as we didn't want people to hate us, but there was nowhere else to throw things.

It was all going very well until we suddenly came to a steep ditch and a stream which we had no means of crossing. Fortunately, some Afghans helped us get over. I stopped smiling then as the bumping really hurt with my back hitting the back of the wheelchair. I made small noises, and Nasrine hissed at me to stop. Being carried makes me feel so weak and I hate it. Soon they put me back down. Some summer rain started falling and I could hear frogs croaking like they were happy and church bells ringing. After travelling for about an hour through the fields we came to the first Macedonian village, Gevgelija. How on earth do you say that? I wondered. We followed a sign marked 'Humanitarian point of the government of Macedonia supported by UNHCR' to an area with lots of white tents and trailers, and a line of smelly Portaloos. UNHCR is the United Nations refugee agency. Crowds of people were gathered waiting. Every so often a man came out with a sheaf of papers and read out names.

When refugees first started pouring into Macedonia, they weren't allowed on public transport, so they had to jump on freight trains or go with smugglers, but some had been mugged by gangs which didn't look good for Macedonia. As a result, in late June the parliament had voted to give SIA refugees three-day visas enabling them to pass through legally and get a train all the way to the Serbian border.

It didn't look like the little police station where we had to get these papers could cope. I guess it had been a very quiet place before. Had we arrived a couple of days later, we would have got completely stuck: because of this bottleneck, the Macedonians ended up blocking the border and firing on and teargassing refugees to stop them coming. We had got through just in time.

Also, because of my wheelchair, we were taken to the front of the queue. We were a little scared about heading off alone as we had been warned about bandits in the forests, and I was saying that Macedonia was the country of Alexander the Great and Genghis Khan (I confused it with Mongolia). Other people think Alexander is a hero, but in my opinion he was a dictator who killed lots of people. Some refugees called the country Mafiadonia and said that it was better to travel in groups for safety, definitely not just two sisters.

Other people were being packed into old trains covered with graffiti. We couldn't imagine getting the wheelchair on. The Macedonian police told us not to worry. After registering us they called a taxi to take us to the border with Serbia for 200 euros, then let us out of the gate at the transit centre. To me this was the Beautiful Gate. We were on our way.

14

Hungary, Open the Door!

Macedonia–Serbia–Hungary, 15–16 September 2015

Macedonia wasn't a big country – we crossed all the way from the south to the north in just two hours. This was just as well because everyone was saying the Hungarians had finished building an enormous fence along their border and at midnight were going to close the gap they had been allowing people through and make it a crime to cross. It was a race against time, like one of those TV shows I'd watched.

First we had to get from Macedonia into Serbia. The taxi drove us about 125 miles and dropped us in the border town of Lojane in the mountains of northern Macedonia. The driver told us that the hills were full of old smuggling routes used for cigarettes, drugs and weapons and it was these that refugees were now using.

Lojane was a village of red-tiled houses with a couple of tea houses and a big white mosque, and the inhabitants were mostly Albanians who had themselves fled from war in their own country in the past. That didn't mean they liked migrants. Some locals were happy because they know we bring in money – they always charge us inflated prices for food and drink – but others complained that we bring crime and infectious disease and frighten their women and kids.

Lots of other refugees were arriving – some like us by taxi and some by train. A camp had been set up in a meadow which they call the Jungle (all migrant camps seem to have the same name), but no one was stopping, even though many had tiredness etched on their faces. We joined what looked like a human highway heading towards the border.

The route was through a cabbage field, which wasn't very easy as it had been raining the night before and it was very muddy. A man was going up and down on a tractor in the next field, a cigarette dangling from his mouth, and some-where a rooster was crowing. Nasrine was struggling with the wheelchair in the mud but some Swiss and Dutch aid-workers handing out energy bars and water bottles spot-ted our predicament and sent four Afghan refugees back to carry me in the chair.

'Welcome to Serbia,' one of the aid-workers said as the men put me down.

'This is the country of famous tennis player Novak Djokovic,' I replied. Nasrine said nothing. I thought about young Gavrilo Princip whose shot started the First World War and Radovan Karadžić, the Bosnian Serb leader responsible for the slaughter of thousands of Muslims in the 1990s – then I was mad at myself as yet again it was always the bad guys I remember! I didn't know anything else about Serbia.

It took us about half an hour to walk across the border to Miratovac, which is the official entry point. Serbian officials checked our papers from Greece and Macedonia. Now we needed a Serbian paper, which took a long time. Nasrine kept looking at her watch. I knew she was trying to work out if we could get to Hungary before nightfall.

When all this crisis started, Serbia had tried to force refugees back to Macedonia, but by the time we came, about 4,000 a day were crossing and the authorities had clearly decided it was easier just to help us on our way. They had even laid on cheap buses to the capital Belgrade, which meant we didn't have to use people smugglers. We followed everyone else uphill along a dusty road where volunteers were handing out water and vegan sandwiches.

It was around 1 p.m. when we got on a bus. We had to pay 35 euros, which was much less than a taxi but it was crowded with immigrants – Syrians like us, as well as Iraqis, Afghans and Eritreans. Disability benefits meant I got to sit at the front.

I stared out of the window. Another country, another language, another culture, none of which we would get to know. It was a long journey, about six hours. I was getting sharp pains in my shoulders and arms and I started worrying I was having a heart attack as I had seen on *Dr Oz* that these can be symptoms. I nudged Nasrine awake to tell her and she was cross. 'You're just exhausted,' she said. 'You won't have a heart attack at sixteen!'

The seats had tables, so I put my head down and tried to sleep but couldn't. Then I tried to lean on Nasrine, but that didn't work either. 'Give me a break,' she muttered.

Belgrade is a big city on the Danube which I was excited to see. We arrived there around 7 p.m. just as normal people were gathering in cafés and bars to wind down from their day's work. They had a kind of hard look maybe because they had had their own civil war in the 1990s. Maybe our life in Syria will go back to some kind of normal one day.

Next stop Hungary and back into the EU if we could get through in time. Nasrine always tells me not to worry about things – she would sort everything out. So I tried not to think about what would happen if we couldn't get through.

Once again we followed everyone else out. There were so many people on the migrant trail we didn't really need the Facebook groups. The park next to the bus station looked like a campsite, full of people and tents amid lines of laundry. Like Basmane Square we could see refugees huddled in negotiations with smugglers on side streets, and cars and vans occasionally pulled up to whisk groups of people towards the Hungarian border.

We had been trying to save money so that Mustafa and Farhad didn't need to keep sending more and planned to get a train. Unlike some refugees who paid smugglers for the whole journey, we were Pay as You Go Migrants. But Nasrine was worried about the time and we found a taxi whose driver said he could take us to the border for 210 euros. Nasrine rested her head against the window like she was sleeping, but the driver spoke some English so I told him, 'I like Novak.' He replied that Djokovic owned a restaurant not far from where we were. I would love to have gone there. Sometimes I wished we weren't doing this journey in such a rush.

It was about 10 p.m. when he dropped us at a small farming town called Horgoš, the same place Bland had come through earlier in the year. I was happy to have crossed two European countries in one day, but it turned out we hadn't been fast enough. Everyone said the border was closed – we were just too late.

There was nothing we could do, so we looked for somewhere to sleep. A lot of people were just huddled in fields, but we didn't want to do that. Around midnight we found a big tent marked with the letters UNHCR. Inside were lots of refugees sleeping so we lay down too. It was very cold and we had no blankets, and I was intimidated because there were a lot of strange people, so didn't really sleep.

When I got up at 8 a.m., everyone was discussing what to do. Breakfast was just an apple someone gave me. Though the border was closed, some women were saying that Hungarian police had let a number of people pass. We thought that, having travelled all this way, we should at least give it a try.

There was supposed to be a bus to Röszke, a few miles away where the crossing was. We waited and waited and were about to give up and get a taxi when the bus came. There was about a half-mile walk from where the bus dropped us to the crossing, along the old railway line, which jolted me in my chair. As we followed everyone – young men, pregnant women, men with children piggybacking – we could see the tall fence that had just been completed with rolls of razor wire on top and we could hear a lot of noise. The gap through which refugees had been entering was closed and people were protesting.

When we got there and saw all the crowds pressed against the fence, with riot police on the other side, that's when for the first time I realized we were in the middle of a big tragedy. Until then I had thought of the journey as an adventure. Now I saw that there was a lot of grief. 'We are escaping war!' someone shouted. To be turned back now after all we had gone through would be unimaginable.

*　*　*

You would think a country like Hungary, which had been cut off from western Europe behind the Iron Curtain until twenty-five years before, would be the last one to build a fence.

But in contrast to the welcome we had received in Serbia, Hungary's right-wing Prime Minister Viktor Orbán really seemed to hate migrants. He kept complaining that migration was fuelling terrorism, and had erected billboards which warned, 'If you come to Hungary don't take the jobs of Hungarians!' and 'If you come to our country you must obey our laws.' Orbán claimed that Hungary was simply trying to enforce EU asylum rules by stopping refugees travelling on. To do this he had erected a 12-foot-high razor-wire fence running along all 110 miles of the border with Serbia, using prisoners to build it.

Until the night we got there they had been allowing people through a gap by the disused railway line, but they had now closed it. We were unlucky. By then around 180,000 refugees had passed through Hungary, just as we had planned to, heading from the border by train or car to Keleti Station in Budapest and from there by car or train to Austria. There were plenty of people smugglers happy to oblige.

About ten days before we got there, Orbán even wrote a newspaper article saying that we migrants threatened Europe's Christian identity. 'Those arriving have been raised in another religion and represent a radically different culture,' he said. 'Most of them are not Christians, but Muslims. This is an important question, because Europe and European identity is rooted in Christianity. Is it not worrying in itself that European Christianity is now barely able to keep Europe Christian? There is no alternative, and we have no option but to defend our borders.'

It wasn't just the government. A Hungarian camerawoman had been filmed deliberately sticking her leg out to trip up a refugee.

Annoyingly, Nasrine told someone I spoke English and suggested that maybe we could use the fact I was in a wheelchair to get them to open the gap again. So I was pushed right to the front facing the gate and the police with helmets and riot shields. Behind me people were shouting 'Germany! Germany!', cursing Hungary and demanding they reopen the border. Some had placards which read 'Europe, Shame'. Others were shouting 'Thank you, Serbia!' I couldn't bear the noise and covered my ears.

Then Hungarian TV pushed a camera at my face. 'If you had Angela Merkel here, what would you say to her?' they asked. 'Help us,' I replied.

I didn't want to say more. I hated the way the wheelchair was being used to try and make Hungarian soldiers feel sorry for me. I hated seeing that the police were wearing white medical masks as if we had infectious diseases.

There was a lot of barbed wire and a little girl with blonde hair standing like a statue with one hand trying to open the gate. 'Hungary, open the door! Hungary, open the door!' she was crying, which broke my heart. 'I want to get out of here,' I told Nasrine.

As the day went on, things got worse. Nasrine wheeled me back along the trail of refugees and discarded rubbish to the main road which was lined with tents, and we watched as a column of armoured vehicles arrived on the Hungarian side. Hundreds more riot police emerged and started turning water cannon and teargas on the people protesting at the border. 'Hungary is a country with a thousand-year-old Christian culture,' Orbán had told the police before sending them off. 'We Hungarians don't want the global-sized movement of people to change Hungary.'

Afterwards the police claimed that 'aggressive' migrants had been breaking through the fence 'armed with pipes and sticks', but we didn't see anything like that, only people throwing plastic water bottles.

I couldn't believe this was the Europe we had dreamt of.

People were saying that, even if you got through the border to the other side, there was nowhere to stay but a muddy field with no facilities. Every so often buses would come and police would herd people on to them to take them to registration camps. Only desperate people would go because everyone was scared of being stuck there or sent back and we'd heard horrible stories of the conditions – that the camps were filthy and full of cockroaches and the guards beat people or forced them to take tranquillizers to keep them quiet. On Facebook you could see secretly filmed footage of guards treating people like animals, throwing food at them. It's funny because actually it costs money to be a refugee. Among us were lawyers, doctors, professors, businessmen. We were human beings, we had had homes before.

Apparently many people were also stuck at Keleti Station, stranded outside, camped out there, with the Hungarian police refusing to let them on to the trains. For a while they even closed it altogether. Some people had been put on a train and told they were going to Austria, only for the train to come to a halt before the border and they were all taken to a camp. Now people were walking.

Everyone was denouncing Hungary. The Austrian Chancellor Werner Faymann even likened what they were doing to the Nazis' deportation of Jews to concentration camps. 'Sticking refugees in trains and sending them somewhere completely different to where they think they're going reminds us of the darkest chapter of our continent's history,' he said.

The whole scene was incredible. This was a country from which around 200,000 people had fled in 1956 after their own failed revolution which Soviet tanks had moved in to crush. Some went across the border we were standing on to what was then Yugoslavia, and most went north to Austria and they were welcomed by their neighbours. I had of course seen a documentary about it which showed all the thank-you notes written by the Hungarians to Austrians about how well they had been treated.

Nasrine pushed me back and forth along the road, but we didn't really know what to do. It seemed we were stranded on the wrong side of the border. We wondered whether to look for smugglers. If we had got across, we had planned to go to a petrol station on the side of the highway where smugglers ply their trade to get a 'taxi' to Budapest. We could see some cars and vans lurking around.

I think the local people felt bad for us. Volunteers were passing out all sorts of food. I watched one little girl devour a can of sweetcorn. I didn't take anything because I was desperate to pee. It wasn't easy finding a place I could use, so I was very careful about how much I drank to make sure I wouldn't cause a problem. Fortunately, I'm a good bladder-keeper.

I tried to focus on other things. One woman was sitting at the roadside crying while breastfeeding a baby in a lilac sleepsuit decorated with fluffy white clouds. It was so tiny she must have had it on the way. Someone said she had lost another child on the train from Macedonia. I know lots of families were being separated and I didn't want to listen because I didn't want my morale to sink any further.

Then a photographer stuck his camera at her and she pulled her veil over her face. There were a lot of journalists at the scene, their satellite trucks and big cars parked all along the road. I know they were trying to do their job of telling the world what was happening, but I guess they don't know that our culture is different. And sometimes it's dangerous. Some of the young men fleeing conscription still had their families back in Syria, so they didn't want their identities revealed.

I noticed the journalists wore a kind of uniform of button-down shirts, jeans and walking boots. I was still wearing the same jeans and favourite denim blue shirt with embroidered shoulders that I had worn from Gaziantep and had not changed since we left Athens. I also noticed they all interviewed the same people, like vultures closing in on prey.

'Hey, there's a Syrian girl in a wheelchair here who speaks English!' I heard somebody shout.

All of a sudden they descended on me. One of them was an American lady from ABC who wanted to know how I knew English. I explained I learnt from watching *Days of Our Lives*. She was astonished.

'That's a great show,' I said. 'But they killed the main character that I loved!'

Another was a nice man from the BBC called Fergal Keane who Nasrine had met on the top deck of the ferry in Athens when she went up to see the sunrise. He had a lovely voice like honey spreading on bread. I told him I wanted to be an astronaut and go into space and find an alien and also go to London to meet the Queen and he laughed a lot.

Hungary, Open the Door!

By then we had lost hope of Hungary opening its doors and someone said the Croatian President had made a speech welcoming refugees. So we could try going that way, and from there through Slovenia. Some of these countries we had never heard of. I heard someone saying people are crossing from Croatia to Slovenia and a man replied, 'That can't be true – Slovenia is in Asia!'

Nasrine pushed me through fields of dead sunflowers, and we got a taxi back the way we had come the night before, then west towards Croatia. It felt like we were in one of those computer games where they keep cutting off routes and you have to find another one.

15

The Hardest Day

Croatia–Slovenia, 16–20 September 2015

I'd never been number one in my life for anything until we went to Slovenia, and of course it turns out it wasn't a good thing.

From the Serbian–Hungarian border, we agreed 125 euros for a taxi back down through Serbia then west to the border with Croatia, a journey of about an hour and a half. Much of that border runs along the River Danube, but there was a crossing place at Apatin on the west bank of the river where we walked through a cornfield into Croatia. I was excited to see another country, even though I felt guilty as it meant more walking and pushing for Nasrine, and happy to see the blue sign with the ring of yellow stars showing that we were back in the EU, so no more borders.

Now we seemed to be on our way again, I tried to chat to Nasrine about my future in Europe. Maybe I would go to school, or even college, and she could help me with physics. Sometimes she likes to talk to me. She says I am a good listener and she can tell me things she tells no one else and I give her wise advice. But I could see she was exhausted and didn't want to talk – I always know when to stay quiet with her.

Once we were over the border Croatian police loaded us into one of those closed vans for transporting prisoners and drove us to a nearby village. There we were put in a bus with other refugees. None of us had any idea where we were going and we heard we were going to be fingerprinted which would have been a disaster as we would have had to stay in Croatia. We were all worried.

The journey was about five hours through the dark and ended in the capital, Zagreb. They took us to a building which seemed like it had been a hospital. There we were each given a number on a piece of paper and photographed holding it up like criminals. Nasrine was number 80 and I was 81. The good thing was there was a shower so we could wash and change. Nasrine washed the clothes we had been wearing since Greece and hung them up to dry. By the time we were done it was about 3 a.m. and finally we slept.

The next day there was a lot of confusion, some people saying we would be fingerprinted. But it didn't happen. Then about midday we were suddenly released. Later we heard that the bus of refugees after us were all fingerprinted, so we were lucky.

We headed out into the city centre, blinking in the sunlight like moles. Zagreb is a beautiful town with grand buildings from the Habsburg Empire. Even the station looks like a palace with a majestic colonnaded façade and a massive statue of King Tomislav, who was Croatia's first king over a thousand years ago and looked a bit grumpy. It turned out there wasn't a train to Slovenia until 4 p.m., so we had three hours to kill. Finally, we might get to see one of the places we were travelling through.

That's when we saw the red sign and golden arch – my first ever McDonald's. By then I was ravenous and I did my best pleading face at Nasrine. I knew she was worried about going to public places. 'OK,' she said.

Of course I had seen all the advertising. I ordered a Big Mac, after checking there was no pork, along with fries and a Coke. The burger came wrapped in paper and the fries in a brown bag instead of on plates. The burger was small and grey, not shining and plump as in the ads, and I had lots of information about how cheap the burger meat was and what it did to your body. So my expectations were not high, but I liked it, particularly with lots of ketchup.

My Coke was bubbly, which I don't really like, and I told Nasrine an interesting fact: that Icelanders consume more

Coca-Cola per capita than any other nation. She wasn't really listening as she was on Google maps trying to figure out our route. It turned out we were not far from Italy. I was excited to go there and see all the famous art and Roman ruins, but it would have been a longer way round than through Slovenia.

Afterwards we went to a shopping mall, my first one, and I had another first too – my first time on an escalator. We spent a long time trying to work out how to use it in a wheel-chair. It was awesome, though a little bit scary on the way down.

Our eyes were on stalks seeing all the shops. Though we don't cover our heads, we always wear clothes with long sleeves and trousers that cover us, so we were still not used to Europe where women show so much flesh. I was happy to be back in a normal life after so long with war and bombing and power-outages. For an hour or so I could pretend I was a girl who lived there rather than a refugee with no home. Nasrine, who had been getting sore eyes from all the dust and pollen, even tried on some sunglasses as if we were just normal shoppers.

That's when we saw a girl looking at us. We were worried, but she was very friendly. 'You are the refugee girl in the photograph in the newspaper!' she said.

'You're famous!' laughed Nasrine. But I was worried that people were just interested in me because of the wheelchair. 'Maybe that's what attracted them,' she said, 'but it's because of your personality they wanted to speak to you.'

The Hardest Day

Sometimes sisters can be sweet as birds even if they support the wrong football team.

Back at the station we heard that Slovenia was stopping trains coming from Croatia. We decided to use some of our precious money to get a taxi instead to the border. We were lucky as the driver's sister lived there, and he knew exactly where to go. The scenery was beautiful. We still couldn't believe how green Europe was. And clean everywhere. It smelled different to Syria, almost as if people perfumed the streets.

The journey west took about an hour and a half, and the driver dropped us near the Slovenian border on an unpronounceable road called Žumberački put. It was strange to think that every country we had been through since leaving Greece had once been one country – Yugoslavia – until just over ten years before. I wondered if our country will end in pieces too.

The taxi driver pointed out a field of flowers through which we had to cross. The sun was setting and we could see nothing ahead but forest and the smudgy purple silhouettes of the mountains. Soon we were in Slovenia. It was weird not seeing any other refugees. There was a small village near by and dogs started barking as we approached. I was mesmerized by the view and loved the feeling of the breeze in my hair and the fresh scent of pines. But Nasrine was terrified. We had nowhere to go and it was getting dark and we'd heard there were bandits robbing refugees – not that we had much. 'Oh God, we're going to have to sleep in the forest,' she said.

That's when we heard footsteps. Some of the locals must have called the police. I think Nasrine was kind of relieved to see them, even though when we said we were from Syria they arrested us. Once again we were loaded into a police van. They took us to a police station in a nearby town called Perišče. Surprisingly in this small place they had an Iraqi translator, and they began this big interrogation asking us how we got through the border and about the whole journey from Syria through Turkey, Greece, Macedonia etc. I couldn't see why they needed to know.

After we had told the whole story, they said we would be fingerprinted. The last thing we wanted was to end up in Slovenia, so we refused. The policeman was insistent. I asked if we were obliged to do it. 'You seem a nice person,' he replied. 'Do you want to do this the easy way or the hard way?' I saw there was no way to avoid it.

That's when we found out we were very unlucky because the Slovenian government had said the first 100 people to enter Slovenia should be interrogated and sent back to Croatia. We were numbers one and two. Typical – the first time in my life I am number one and it's a bad thing!

By then it was very late, so we were locked in a cell with bars in the police station and told we would be sent back to Croatia the next day. The cell had two bunks and a button for calling the guard if we needed anything. I wasn't happy to be in jail, but I was so tired that it was the first time for ages that I had a good sleep.

Next morning we waited and waited. They'd told us we would be picked up at 9 a.m., but it got to 1 p.m. and nobody told us anything. Eventually we called the guard. He said the Croatian government had refused to take us back.

Then we were taken outside to a yard where a lot of other refugees were being held. They told us they had come by train from Croatia and been locked inside the carriages for hours and eventually brought there. There was an officer from UNHCR and he said to me we should apply for asylum there in Slovenia. I got mad and told him, 'You are supposed to protect refugees! We are two young girls alone in a foreign city, we are not going to stay here alone, waiting for months. What would happen to us?'

Finally, a tour bus arrived and we were told to get on with the other refugees. As usual we were sitting at the front. Yet again we had no idea where we were going. There were other Syrians on the bus as well as Afghans, but most seemed to be Iraqis, including a group of Yazidis. Not only had they travelled the journey we had made, but they had first had to cross Syria. We felt bad for them because they had had to cross through two war zones, and at the end of their journey it was only Syrians who the Germans had said they would accept.

The bus drove through kind of Alpine scenery with forested mountains, waterfalls, lakes and sheer cliffs dotted with trees. The road signs were not much help in revealing where we were going as the words were incomprehensible and looked as if they were missing vowels, but some people were following on Google maps and said we were heading west towards the capital Ljubljana.

Dusk was falling as we drew up at the Postojna Centre for Foreigners, a two-storey building with bars on the windows that looked very scary and turned out to be a military camp. Policemen boarded the bus and announced that they would take our phones, money and valuables. Everyone got very worried. 'They are going to lock us in here, otherwise why would they take the phones?' said one man.

'We are not getting off the bus!' someone shouted.

I guess the Iraqis were Shias because they started saying prayers to Ali – I'd never heard Shias praying before. We Sunnis say, 'There is no God but Allah, whose prophet is Muhammad (PBUH),' but the Shias added an extra phrase at the end: 'and Ali is the friend of God'. I tried not to listen as we are not polytheist.

Hearing them reminded me of watching the Royal Wedding on TV in Aleppo. Nasrine was cleaning the room at the time, and when Prince William and Kate started saying the marriage vows and exchanged rings they said, 'in the name of the Father, and of the Son, and of the Holy Ghost'. I didn't understand as I didn't know about Christianity at the time, but Nasrine said, 'Ignorant people!'

The Shias praying and moaning scared us. Nasrine started crying. Then someone said he knew a person who had been locked up in the camp for two months, at which everyone freaked out. People started asking what guarantee there was that we could leave once inside.

Finally, the policemen ran out of patience and ordered us out of the bus, then herded us inside the detention centre. Although they let us keep our phones, there was no signal or wifi, so we couldn't see where we were. I started crying because I thought I would never see sunlight again.

But then I thought that these are the kind of obstacles I will face in a new country, and I started calming myself down. I thought of Nelson Mandela and the twenty-seven years he had spent in jail, never losing his spirit, and Abdullah Öcalan, leader of the Kurdish PKK, who has been in jail in Turkey since 1999. But they were not ideal for cheering you up, so then I tried to focus on listing Romanov rulers which usually works.

Inside the centre we were divided into two groups – single men and families. Nasrine and I were taken to a room with an Afghan family. The woman was veiled and there was a man and a little boy, and we couldn't understand a word they said. We were a bit scared of Afghans after the fight they had caused in Lesbos and also because they always refused to queue at the border points. Sometimes they pretended to be

Syrians to try and get through borders as it was Syrians the Germans had said they would accept, but we couldn't believe anyone would be convinced as their language and appearance was completely different.

Then we heard someone speaking Arabic outside, a Syrian man complaining to a guard that his wife shouldn't be in the same room as a foreign man. After that the guard came in and took away the Afghans and brought the Syrians in instead.

They were from Idlib in northern Syria, which after a big battle was no longer under Assad's control and had been taken over by the al-Nusra Front. The group comprised a married man, his wife and baby, her brother and a single mother who said she had come alone because her husband had been killed in a bombing raid. She showed us photographs on her phone of her children who she had left in a camp in Lebanon. As she couldn't take them all to Germany her plan was to make her way there alone, request asylum, then get them out through family reunification. A lot of people seemed to be doing that, but we knew from Bland it wasn't so easy.

The Idlib family were nice, but I was too exhausted to listen to any more sad stories. It was a rough night. There were six bunk beds, and my sister and I took one pair, me in the lower and Nasrine above. They were uncomfortable and I was scared of rolling out, and a mosquito kept bothering me. I dreamt of Ayee, that I was sleeping next to her, but when I tried to roll close to her I woke and saw she wasn't there, which upset me. Then we were woken at 4 a.m. as the other family had set the alarm on their phone to pray.

Nasrine said when she heard the beeping in her sleep she started dreaming that she was on a pilgrimage like our Haj in Mecca, only in Slovenia and with everyone dressed in white. She usually prays every day and I guess she was feeling guilty that she wasn't praying on the journey.

After breakfast of bread and cheese we went outside. There was a yard where some of the refugees were playing football, and it had netting all around and over the top, so it felt as if even the sky was locked out. That was the scariest part for me. I thought, I'm a prisoner here.

Inside was a big hall with a TV which was showing Al Jazeera. The main news was the refugee crisis – a 'tidal wave of humanity' they called us – and we watched to see what was happening on the borders. We saw that Hungary was still closed and more and more people were streaming into Croatia – 11,000 so far – and it had closed almost all road crossings and was saying it couldn't accept any more people. Slovenia had stopped all rail traffic on the main line from Croatia and said it was going to introduce border controls. Even Germany was so overwhelmed it had suspended trains from Austria. There was footage of people stampeding for a bus to Croatia and others swarming across fields. It was like we were a lost tribe being pushed from border to border.

The report then switched to Brussels, where EU leaders in suits kept having meetings to discuss the 'migrant crisis'.

They all agreed it was very serious and something needed to be done, but none of them seemed to want us and everyone seemed very cross with Germany. I couldn't help thinking that there might be a lot of us but even if we were a million we were not even 0.2 per cent of the 500 million living in the EU, and in our tradition we would never turn away those in need.

'The European Union is not in a good situation,' said a serious man with glasses called Jean-Claude Juncker, whose head stuck out like my old tortoise, and who was described as President of the European Commission (I wasn't sure what that was). 'There is a lack of Europe in this Union and a lack of union in this Union.' I wondered why he didn't do something if he was in charge. Instead it was like the rest of the world just wished we would go away.

All anybody talked about was the migration crisis. A lot of the people at the centre were from Aleppo like us but had left more recently and had terrible stories to tell of the bombing and the hunger.

Nasrine spoke to the Yazidis – their dialect is similar to the Kurmanji we speak. There was one girl whose two brothers had been killed by Daesh as they fled the mountains and her sister kidnapped. She and others who escaped had scratched their faces to make themselves ugly to Daesh so they wouldn't be taken. Her parents had sold everything they had left including her mother's gold to enable her to leave. 'There is nothing good for us in Iraq,' she said. She had tattooed her name on her wrist in case she was killed and no one knew who she was.

We also met a Palestinian family with six children, including two pairs of twins, who told us they were two-times refugees – their family had fled to Syria in 1948 after the British Mandate in Palestine ended and Jewish militias started razing villages to seize land for the new state of Israel. We used to have about half a million Palestinians in Syria because of course it was once a good place to live.

This family had grown up in a big camp just south of Damascus called Yarmouk which was like a city with schools, hospitals and even its own newspapers. They had tried to stay out of the revolution, but in 2012 the regime decided the area was becoming a haven for rebel fighters so it was bombed by Assad's jets. Daily gun battles erupted between both sides and they fled to a camp in Lebanon. Life there, they said, was miserable – Palestinians don't get the same treatment as Syrians and they had to pay for residency permits and rent in the camp. Initially they thought Assad would soon be ousted and they could go back to Yarmouk. But that didn't happen. As time went on and more refugees came, sympathy for them in Lebanon wore thin. Now there are 1.2 million Syrians there – equivalent to almost a quarter of their population – and it's only a small strip of land.

The family's money was running low, as were food rations in the camp. When they heard Mrs Merkel's words and saw that people were getting to Germany, they decided to try themselves.

They paid smugglers to get them to Turkey and from there crossed on a boat to Greece, to the island of Kos. It sounded as though conditions there were worse than Lesbos as the mayor hated refugees and locked them in a football stadium with no water. Finally, they got the official papers and booked a ferry to Athens. Like ours it was leaving in the early hours and they all fell asleep. When they woke up the next morning they saw the ferry hadn't moved. People were so angry there were riots. Eventually the ferry left. After eight hours it stopped and they got off. Only then did they realize they were now in Mitilini in Lesbos, not Athens.

As they told the story they laughed a lot. Refugees are resilient people.

I was surprised how calm Nasrine was. Maybe it was because the Idlib family had promised they would accompany us to Germany so we wouldn't be alone.

For me it was the hardest day of the trip. We'd lost everything – our country, our home, my aunt and uncle – and been separated from our family, and now we were prisoners. It's actually illegal to lock up refugees, but what could we do? I was scared we would be kept there for three or four months.

There, surrounded by police and not able to get out, I realized how precious freedom is and how valuable it is to be free.

The Hardest Day

That was the day I understood why we had started this whole revolution, even though Assad had responded by leading the country to its destruction. No longer could I pretend I was on some sort of holiday trip across Europe – now I knew I was truly a refugee.

The only good thing about the detention centre was the food, in particular a red rosehip drink called Cockta that tasted of herbs and petals and reminded me of the sarep I loved when I was a child.

But then we heard that the Iraqis had got out by going on a hunger strike, and we decided to do the same. The threat worked and finally the next day – after two nights – the Slovenians let us go and put us on a bus to an open camp in a place called Logatec.

Only as we were leaving Postojna did I realize how beautiful it was, surrounded by nature, hills, where everything was green. Later I looked the place up and read that baby dragons had been born in a cave in those mountains just above where we were. I didn't even know there were actually dragons. I felt sorry that all we were seeing of countries were police and refugees.

16

The Sound of Music

Slovenia–Austria, 20–21 September 2015

I was a bit scared entering Austria for two reasons. One, as I told Nasrine, it was where Hitler was born, the man who caused Europe's last really big refugee crisis. Secondly, it was where seventy-one refugees had died the previous month, suffocated inside a truck meant for transporting frozen chickens. The truck had been abandoned at the side of a motorway from Budapest to Vienna and was spotted by Austrian police because it had liquid seeping out the back. When they opened it, the smell of death was overpowering for it was piled up with rotting corpses, including eight women, three children and a baby of just eighteen months, and there were dents in the sides of the truck where the desperate people must have been banging as they ran out of oxygen.

On our journey, apart from the leg between Turkey and Greece, we had tried to avoid smugglers, though we had been overcharged by many taxis. But generally we had been lucky, maybe because of disability benefits, and for the most part people along the way had tried to help us. We knew many refugees had walked hundreds of miles. Only in Turkey and Greece had we spent nights sleeping outside. Sometimes we joked that we were five-star refugees.

We were so near now to the end – just one more country to cross – that we didn't want to risk anything. Austria had put border controls back in place and one of our cousins had told us that Austria was sending refugees to a detention centre to reduce pressure on Germany. So we decided that we would get off the train from Logatec to Austria one stop before the border in case police got on and arrested people there.

The train was going to the Austrian town of Graz and we got off at the last Slovenian town, which was Maribor. The Idlib family, who we had travelled with from the detention centre, thought we were foolish and stayed on board. As Nasrine wheeled me out, several people tried to stop us, crying, 'This is not Austria, it's Slovenia!'

'I know,' I replied. I thought the plan was stupid, because we looked awful and tired and people would wonder what we were doing and be suspicious.

Austria is so near that many people in Maribor cross the border every day for work, but it turned out that it's still about 14 miles away, so not exactly walking distance as we had thought. We started along the highway looking for a taxi. We looked so pathetic that I think if people had seen us they would have cried.

We quickly discovered that our plan really was stupid because some volunteers stopped with a car laden with food for refugees, and they told us there was no way by road or foot to avoid the police on the border – the best way was by train. Then the Idlib family called us and said they had got through to Graz with no problem. So we had chosen the wrong option.

The volunteers called a taxi for us. The driver charged us half price because we were refugees. We realised we had crossed the whole of Slovenia almost for free. Not everyone hates us.

As it always seemed to be wherever we went into a new country, it was near sunset when we entered Austria. I was confused as there was no sign to show we were in a different country – no flag, nothing.

The taxi left us at a police barrier in a place called Spielfeld where there were lots of tents and some volunteers from the Red Cross and the Order of Malta. An interpreter who spoke Arabic in an Egyptian dialect directed us to a tent where we were given a sandwich and a blanket and told there would be a bus later to a camp in Graz. I didn't like the place as it was very cold and there weren't even mattresses, and there weren't enough tents so some people were having to sleep outside. Someone said we were free to leave, but if we got caught we could be fingerprinted and end up forced to request asylum in Austria. We didn't know what to do.

There were crowds of people there and some told us they had been waiting for the bus since 8 a.m. We waited and waited and thought we might have to spend the night there. I was completely exhausted and shivering. Finally, at midnight the bus arrived. We were driven to Graz, which was the birthplace of Archduke Franz Ferdinand. I knew this because once I watched a programme on the Most Important Assassinations in history. I was convinced that number one would be Mahatma Gandhi, but it turned out to be Archduke Ferdinand because of course they judged the killing by the impact it had on the world. How stupid I was!

We got off the bus at the camp and translators in bright orange safety vests shouted at us in different languages through megaphones to queue up. Some of these refugees were lawyers, doctors or important people in their communities back home, but standing there exhausted with their few belongings in rucksacks, duffle bags and shopping bags everyone looked grim and beaten down.

We were divided between those wanting to stay in Austria and those hoping to go on to Germany, which was almost everyone.

Each person, including children and babies, was given a green wristband. I was shocked as it made me think of the way Nazis made Jews wear yellow badges, but the volunteers explained that we needed them to get food. The bands had numbers and when ours were called we would then board a bus taking us to the Austria–Germany border. We were numbers 701 and 702, which meant we might be there a very long time as each bus only took forty people, and we were told only four or five were going a day. It's funny, Austria is a rich country but it seemed even they couldn't cope with the numbers.

After receiving our wristbands, we were taken into the refugee centre which was in a former supermarket. Before we left Turkey I had learnt a few words of German in preparation, so I tried asking one of the volunteers for hot tea. I was given cold milk. There were extension cords dangling down near the entrance and like everyone the first thing we did was charge our phone for that was our lifeline.

Inside there were row upon row of green metal fold-up beds like army cots or for medical examinations. Almost every bed had someone lying on it. There must have been a thousand people there. It was completely enclosed and very crowded, the air stale with so many people who hadn't washed for days or weeks, like us. It was also bright with big strip-lights. We were shown to two cots and volunteers offered us each a heavy grey blanket or *Decke* – the first new German word I learnt.

We were trying to sleep when angry shouting erupted. A group of Afghan and Syrian men were fighting over the power outlets in the charging area. I realized how terrible our behaviour had become because of the war.

The lights were suddenly switched off and I tried to sleep but it was hard with so many children crying, and it was also cold. The tent had just one heater, which clearly wasn't enough to warm the whole place, and the blankets were not enough. Nasrine took out all the clothes we had in the rucksack to spread over me, but I was still cold and my teeth were aching.

The camp was being run by the Austrian army and soldiers came to clean the tent in the morning, collecting water bottles and rubbish.

While we were waiting, Nasrine started chatting to people on neighbouring cots. I didn't really talk to them of course as I always closed my ears to the bad things. Some discussed which places to go to – whether to try Sweden, Denmark or Holland as Germany was getting full. Others told fragments of their stories.

One of them was a beautiful girl called Hiba a few years older than me and she was in tears because she had been separated from her boyfriend in Hungary. She was an economics student from Damascus and had left with her brothers and her boyfriend's family after her elder brother had been conscripted and killed in the war. They had been travelling in a big group, but they had an awful time in Hungary, stuck for days at Keleti Station. They then used a smuggler to get to the Austrian border only to be sent back. At the border they heard about the people suffocated in the truck just one day earlier. After that her boyfriend's family decided to give up and go to a Hungarian camp and ask for asylum there. He had no choice but to go with them. She and her brothers decided to make their way back to Budapest and use another smuggler to go on to Austria. This time they succeeded. Now she was sending the boy messages on Facebook Messenger and he was not replying. All she had was a pink fluffy bear he had left her. Describing how she had watched him being driven away in the Hungarian police bus, she said, 'Goodbyes are not cool.' It was like *Romeo and Juliet*, or *Mem and Zin*.

When I went to the toilet I saw a lot of veiled women but also one Syrian girl with long blonde hair who looked European. She told us that people were getting stuck in the camp for two or three days waiting for the buses. I couldn't imagine staying in that dreadful place for three days so we tried to use my asthma as an excuse. We went to the first-aid centre and told the doctor I couldn't stay there as it was too claustrophobic, but he said we would have to wait.

Then a volunteer called out the numbers for the next bus. They were much lower than ours. Dozens of refugees surged towards the gates that, when opened, would lead them to the bus taking them to the German border. People were pushing to get on, even though it was not their turn, while volunteers in their orange vests tried to keep the crowd back.

I was desperate to get out of that place. Refugees live on rumours and Facebook messages and we heard that trains were running again from Austria to Germany. Someone told us that if you had money you could get taxis to Graz station and catch a train, so we decided to do that despite our fears of being picked up and fingerprinted.

Our driver was Egyptian and he started telling us about the impact of the refugees suddenly arriving – refugees were walking along the highway and the Austrians didn't know what to do. He said it was as if foreign plants had suddenly grown: everything they did was different. We kept laughing at the idea of us as exotic plants.

Because of the wheelchair someone helped us on to a train. Once we were inside some other Syrians tried to talk to us, but we shrugged them off because if police did come on board we didn't want to look like a refugee group.

Nasrine was relieved we were now almost in Germany. 'Now this really looks like western Europe,' she said.

Being so close to our final destination made me happy and sad at the same time. Europe was exactly as I had pictured in my dreams – the nature, the green – even though of course I prefer my homeland. We couldn't believe how clean the streets were. The Egyptian taxi driver had told us that in Austria you have to pay a fine if you throw cigarette packs out of car windows like people do all the time in Syria.

But I was sad that our journey was almost concluded and that I would go back to being the girl in her room. For the last three weeks I had felt like everyone else, experiencing real-life events, even if I had needed my sister to push me.

As we chugged through the Alps, past snow-topped mountains and little villages with wooden chalets and churches with onion-shaped domes, I thought of Heidi living with her cranky grandfather and Peter the goatherd. I often read that book because not many books have disabled characters, but Heidi has an invalid friend Clara who comes to stay, which makes Peter jealous. He tosses her wheelchair down the mountain, then she learns to walk in the healthy Alpine air. Also I love the bit when Heidi rescues a basketful of kittens from the clock-tower of Clara's grand house and the house-keeper screams. I would have screamed too.

The green meadows made me think of *The Sound of Music* and Maria skipping across them in her governess pinafores. I couldn't help imagining her as she was in the film which was annoying because I had read *The Story of the Trapp Family Singers*, the book of the real Maria von Trapp, and the movie ruined it.

By the way, I know the names of all the real children in *The Sound of Music* – the oldest was a boy called Rupert, not a girl called Liesl – and there were ten of them not seven. Also Captain von Trapp wasn't stern like in the movie, and he played the violin not the guitar. It's like Syria and Assad, the way we are always being deceived by people at the top.

The von Trapps were refugees too, fleeing Austria after the Nazis had taken it over in 1938. They also went by train – not fleeing over the mountains as in the film. They went on a concert tour from which they never returned. They then travelled by boat to New York, and when they arrived they had only a few dollars to their name.

That was a familiar story – though in our case of course we were fleeing to Germany not away from it. It was lucky we were almost in Germany, for we too had almost run out of money, having exhausted all the funds our brothers Mustafa and Farhad had sent.

When the train drew into Salzburg, police got on the train and made all Syrians get off. We realized then that there were hundreds of us. So much for our attempts to avoid drawing attention. The station was also full of refugees – so many had turned up when Hungary closed their doors and the new route opened from Slovenia that the mayor had to turn the underground car park into a camp. It looked well organized, with beds and first aid and a children's play area. There were even local people holding signs saying 'Wilkommen' and 'Welcome Refugees' and handing out pears and bananas.

We were directed to a bus which drove us to a military base near a bridge over the River Saalach. There once again police boarded and told us to get out. Austrian soldiers then gave us water and biscuits. Finally, we were given a signal and walked in small clusters of twenty over the bridge into Germany. Well, I didn't walk. I wish I could. Maybe I need a Peter to toss away my wheelchair.

On the way across someone gave me a packet of gummi bears. When we got to the other side, we didn't know where to go, but someone had scrawled 'Germani' on the ground in orange chalk as well as orange arrows, like something from *Hansel and Gretel*, guiding us as if Germany was our home. However, there were no German flags, so we weren't sure whether we had arrived.

'Where is Germany?' I asked a policeman.

He smiled. 'Welcome to Germany,' he said.

17

Thank You, Mama Merkel

Rosenheim, Dortmund, Essen, Germany, 21 September–
15 October 2015

The day we entered Germany was Nasrine's twenty-sixth birthday. The journey from Gaziantep had taken exactly a month, and the undersides of my arms were covered in bruises from banging against the wheelchair. But we had made it. Since leaving Aleppo, we had travelled more than 3,500 miles across nine countries from war to peace – a journey to a new life, like my name.

Suddenly everything had become *when*, not *if*. I looked at the Germans and thought that one day I will speak like them, live like them, love like them. Maybe even walk like them. We called Ayee and Yaba to tell them we had arrived and they cried, and we called Bland to say we would see him soon. We were crying too, and so were some of the other refugees. It was like a big weight had been lifted. We didn't know what would happen next, but we had reached our geographical goal.

First, though, we had to wait, for once we had crossed the Saalach bridge into Freilassing in Germany there were people everywhere on both sides of the road. The police instructed us to go down under the bridge and line up. There was a long queue of Syrians, Iraqis, Afghans, Pakistanis and some really black-skinned people who I guess had come from Africa.

'I am going to the front. I can't stay like this in this long line,' I told the policeman. But this time disability benefits didn't work. He looked at the gummi bears I had been given. 'You are a Muslim, right?' he asked. 'Yes,' I replied. 'Give me the sweets,' he said. 'They are full of gelatine.'

Then we were left to wait. We were given nothing to drink and it started getting colder. This wasn't quite the welcome we had imagined.

We ended up under that bridge for five hours. That might not seem a lot of time after all those weeks of travel and the years of Assad or Taliban or whatever monsters we were fleeing, but it was hard to be so close to the end and then get stuck for no reason we could see.

Finally, we were told to come back up to the bridge. Our bags were checked and we were loaded into a police bus and driven through more Heidi mountains and forests and past a lake of ice-blue water to a town around 50 miles to the west called Rosenheim in Bavaria.

The camp was inside a kind of closed market. Just as in Austria, we were given numbered wristbands, this time in red, and told that our numbers would be called when it was our turn to board a bus to the next stage. Nasrine and I got bands 12 and 13, so we thought we were among the first, but it turned out there were 300 green, 300 blue and 100 orange in front of us. Then they told us they could only handle fifty a day, so we might be there for days.

Just as we had imagined about Germany, everything was very organized. We were directed to what they called Bearbeitungsstrasse or Processing Street in a sports hall. They gave us plastic bags for our phones and valuables, photographed us and checked us for contagious diseases like TB and scabies. I do understand the need to register every-one but, honestly, we're not a disease or an epidemic. Still, I can't complain because at least in Germany the door was open, unlike some other EU countries.

Lastly we were fingerprinted. It was strange to no longer need to be scared of fingerprinting. They gave us a document called an *Anlaufbescheinigung*, which meant we could travel on to Munich to apply for asylum.

We didn't want to go to Munich as Dortmund was where Bland lived. I told them, 'I don't want to stay here, I want to see my brother,' but they said Munich was the official entry point for refugees. The problem was, it was overwhelmed with around 13,000 arriving every day.

That meant more waiting. The market camp was crowded with hundreds of people on cots looking bored. There was an area with toys like Lego and teddy bears that people had donated, but many of the children were crying, tired of being dragged along and cooped up. The heat was suffocating and people were collapsing – we saw a woman faint in the bathroom. There were long queues just to get a sandwich.

For the first time we met people who had come on the other route by sea to Italy. Their trips across the Mediterranean from Libya to a tiny island called Lampedusa in rickety fishing boats sounded terrifying. Many boats had capsized and hundreds of people drowned in the open sea.

A lot of people like us were trying to go to different places in Germany where they already had family. Eventually, with the assistance of a volunteer who felt sorry for us, we managed to hide our wristbands and get on an earlier bus. This one was going to another camp in a town called Neumarkt, not far from Nuremberg. There we were once again told to give our names and register. We didn't want to get stuck, so we said we were going outside for some fresh air. Across the road was a petrol station and they called a taxi to take us to Nuremberg.

Nuremberg is a very pretty town with colourfully painted buildings like gingerbread houses and turrets on whirligig towers as if from a fairytale. We stared into the windows of bakers with the gooey chocolate cakes and *Apfelstrudel* I had read about. Nasrine said she felt glad we had done the journey the way we had because going through a lot of countries had given us time to adapt, whereas if we had just flown by plane straight to somewhere like that in Germany we would have been completely bewildered. I agreed: we would have been stunned.

Then we saw another McDonald's and I had my first fast-food meal in my new country. As we ate my eyelids started to droop. Suddenly I felt terribly exhausted. I had done my best and come to the right place, and now I just wanted to be done with travelling. The plan was to take a train to Cologne where our eldest brother Shiar lived, then go and apply for asylum the next morning. There was a fast train at 9 p.m. which we had just enough money left for. At the station we were amazed by the lifts and everything designed to make life easier for disabled people. As Nasrine says, everything is different in Germany.

In our carriage were two Afghan men who started praying, their heads bobbing up and down, and chanting 'Allahu Akbar'. We were a bit scared and could see Germans on the train looking alarmed. That was the first time I thought about what Germans might think of us refugees coming to live in their country in such numbers.

Not everyone in Bavaria had been happy to see the state become the gateway for tens of thousands of refugees entering Europe's top economy. The state premier Horst Seehofer was warning of 'an emergency situation we soon won't be able to control'. His party's vice president, Hans-Peter Friedrich, predicted 'catastrophic consequences' and speculated that jihadists from Daesh could be hiding among us.

Fortunately, Mrs Merkel is a feisty lady. 'If we have to start apologizing for showing a friendly face in an emergency, that's not my country,' she said.

Thank you, Mama Merkel.

The train journey was about four hours and we ended up alongside the Rhine just next to Cologne Cathedral, which was tall, dark and brooding and seemed to fill the whole skyline. I'd never seen such a massive church. Once it was the tallest building in the world. How did that not get destroyed in the war?

And then we were pulling into the platform and there was Bland waiting for us with his floppy hair and soppy grin. He had travelled from Dortmund to meet us. I couldn't believe we were back together. I was so happy to see him – he has been part of every event in my life.

When we got to Shiar's house Nahda was also there with her kids – she had waited for us to arrive so that we could apply for asylum together. It felt so good and homey for us all to be back together. I thought that the start of our new life had begun. I didn't know what it would be and desperately needed familiar things and people around me.

*　*　*

Next morning, we three sisters, two brothers and my four nieces all took a train to Dortmund. The train went through Düsseldorf. I'd never seen so many tall glass buildings, glittering in the rain. I didn't look for long, though. I was so happy to be back with Bland I couldn't stop looking at him.

He showed us three sisters and Nahda's children to the office of what the Germans call BAMF, the Federal Office for Migration and Refugees, which was crowded with other refugees.

'We are Syrians,' we told the receptionist. We were sent to have our photographs taken, then we waited for our turn to go to a counter and fill out an application form for asylum. Among the questions was a list of diseases or conditions to tick if you suffered them. Cerebral palsy was not on the list so Shiar suggested I write on the end, '*Ich kann nicht laufen*' – German for I cannot run.

The assistant told us that because of the backlog it would be about three months before our asylum interview. Bland had put his application in on 15 July in Bremen and was still in a camp in Dortmund waiting for his. In the meantime we would be sent to a camp while they tried to arrange more permanent accommodation. They explained that normally asylum seekers are sent on to a camp the same day, but in our case as I was a minor and our parents were not with us we would have to wait in the registration centre overnight.

They put us in a bare room with just bunk beds and lots of graffiti on the walls. Shiar and Bland were not allowed to stay and were sent away, which I hadn't expected. It felt like no sooner had we been reunited than we were parted.

The following day I had an interview with the person responsible for minors who asked if I wanted to stay with my brother and sisters or become a ward of the German authorities and go to what they called a minors' camp. Stupid question! Though later I found out that minors' camps had much better conditions and I teased Nasrine that I should have gone to one and enjoyed comfy beds, chocolate ice-creams and TV.

After my interview we were told we had to wait till 2 p.m. to find out where we were going. Germany distributes refugees across the country in proportion to the population and tax revenue of its sixteen provinces, using a system called the *Königsteiner Schlüssel*. Those provinces then distribute them among their cities and towns, which get funding from federal, state and local government to provide housing and other services. The problem was that there were so many of us that local authorities were struggling to cope. Municipalities were being given less than forty-eight hours' notice to find accommodation for hundreds of refugees. They were using sports centres, stadiums, school gyms, day-care centres, office space, even the old Nazi-built airport in Berlin, and erecting tennis bubbles in parks or on sports fields. In Cologne they were even buying luxury hotels.

Thank You, Mama Merkel

The province we were in was North Rhine-Westphalia, which was getting more than 20 per cent of all refugees. It was said to be an easier place to be a refugee, and the people there were used to foreigners because in the 1960s and 1970s many Kurds from Turkey had settled in the province as there was lots of industry which needed workers. So there was less racism. That's why Shiar had settled there and also our uncle. And it has a woman premier.

Finally, our names were announced and they said we would be going to a camp in Essen on a bus at 4.15 p.m.

The bus left at 4.30 p.m. – late by German standards. Uncle Ahmed and Aunt Shereen, with whom we had taken the boat to Lesbos, were in a camp in Essen, so we were excited we would be in the same place. We started following our journey on the Google map and could see we were getting closer and closer to their camp, but then our bus turned off.

The camp we were taken to was a former hospital, and they gave us a room on the ground floor for me, Nahda, Nasrine and Nahda's daughters. Medical staff came and checked our hair for lice, gave vaccines to the children and took blood. In my case when they put in the syringe, no blood would come. The nurse said it was because I was dehydrated as I had hardly been eating or drinking along the journey, and she said I must eat. But the food was terrible, so as usual I didn't eat. I'm fussy at the best of times and Nasrine gets very cross as all I will drink is tea. If she changes one ingredient in a dish I like I always notice and won't eat it.

The first morning, Nasrine went off to get me breakfast and came back looking astonished. Another cousin of ours called Mohammed was in the queue – we had last seen him in Manbij.

After all our experiences on this trip I had got used to being in a camp and having lots of people around, but it was boring, particularly because I mostly stayed in the room. There was a small yard which Nasrine pushed me round for some fresh air and there was a daily German lesson at 2 p.m., but they taught only basic things like numbers, days and months which I had already learnt.

We ended up in Essen for twenty days. We were worrying about where they would send us. We heard they were running out of space for refugees and were worried we might end up sleeping in a sports hall. I used the disabled card to ask to speak to the head of camps and explained I couldn't live in a stadium, and anyway we wanted to go to Wesseling near Cologne as our brother was there and could help us.

On 28 September, after we had been there for four days, I was feeling really down. I'd thought we would arrive in Germany and I would go to school and instead I was stuck in a camp. That morning Nasrine and Nahda had gone to a room where donated clothes were handed out, and they left me watching the kids. They were very naughty and I had nothing but my voice to control them with and ended up screaming at them. It made me feel how weak and useless I was, and I burst into tears.

Then Nasrine came in holding her phone and said she had a surprise for me.

'What is it – Masoud Barzani [the President of Iraqi Kurdistan] wants to speak to me?' I joked.

'No,' she replied. 'Look at this.'

She opened a link to show me a video. It was an American TV show called *Last Week Tonight* hosted by a British man called John Oliver and he was talking about refugees. Annoyingly, the wifi in the camp was very slow with so many refugees using it and the video kept stopping. Then he showed me talking to the BBC reporter Fergal Keane about wanting to be an astronaut and meet the Queen. I almost dropped the phone.

John Oliver explained how I had learnt English from *Days of Our Lives* and was sad about EJ being killed off. 'How can you not want this girl in your country?' he asked. 'She would improve any country that would have her.' I couldn't believe he was talking about me. But that wasn't all. He talked about the bad situation faced by refugees, the way the British Prime Minister David Cameron had called us a 'swarm', how Denmark was taking out ads in Lebanese papers saying 'Don't come', and the hostility in Hungary including the camerawoman sticking out her foot.

Then he said we have a surprise for one refugee. They showed film of a man's hand ringing a doorbell. The person opening the door was Sami from *Days of Our Lives* and as she opened it, the man standing there was EJ! 'No way!' she screamed. I screamed too. Then of course they embraced. EJ explained that after he'd been shot, his sister had rescued him from the morgue, flown him to Germany and witchdoctors had performed magic to resurrect him.

'I can't imagine how horrible that was for you,' said Sami.

'Coming back from the dead is not hard,' he replied. 'You know what's hard – getting from Syria to Germany.' He talked a little about the migrant crisis. Then he said he had read about 'this incredible sixteen-year old from Kobane called Nujeen Mustafa'.

'Nujeen Mustafa.' Sami repeated my name like it was something wondrous.

I was totally astonished, yelling and screaming. My favourite characters on my favourite soap opera far away in America talking about me. They brought someone back from the dead for a Syrian refugee! Also I didn't expect to see them in love again.

Shortly afterwards I got a call from a lady in America to ask me if I liked the video. Of course, I said. Then she said the actors, Alison Sweeney and James Scott, who play Sami and EJ, would like to talk to me. When they came on the phone I was so excited I didn't know what to say. I told them how the first thing I had done when I got internet in Turkey was

Google them and I knew Alison was married with two children. I said the show was flavourless without them. I probably sounded like a silly fan.

Nasrine was in shock. 'For three years you have been going on about these people in an American soap opera,' she said. 'Now they are chasing you. How on earth did they reach you?'

The next day I watched it again, then made a video message from our small room and posted it on YouTube. 'This is my lucky day,' I said. 'And in my lucky day I have something to say to the victims of the wars around the world. You are stronger and braver than you think. Also thank everyone for supporting me during my journey. Wish me luck and good luck for you!'

Yet the following morning I woke and felt as if something had been stolen from me. *Days of Our Lives* had been my own thing, it was private. Also the video clip wasn't realistic – EJ and Sami would have had a fight. I would have liked that better than them talking about me.

PART THREE

A Normal Life

Germany, 2015–

After all, tomorrow is another day.

Scarlett O'Hara in *Gone With the Wind*, Margaret Mitchell

18

Foreigners in a Foreign Land

Nobody leaves their home without a reason. Sometimes I wake in the middle of the night with nightmares about the bombing and reach for my mum and she is not there and I feel sad. But after two or three minutes I think, Nujeen, you are still alive and far from bombing, everything is OK. Here in Germany, I feel safe. You can go for a walk and don't expect to be dead by morning. There's no bombing, no tanks, no army, no Daesh on the street.

On 1 November we moved into our new home which is the ground floor of a two-storey German house on a suburban street in a small town called Wesseling, 10 miles south of Cologne. It's made of concrete and bricks rather than gingerbread and is brown and cream rather than pink or blue, but to me it still feels like Disneyland, the kind of place I always dreamt of living in.

We have a living room, a small shower room, a kitchen and just two bedrooms, which is quite tight for us three sisters and the four children, particularly as Bland often stays with us. But it is ours – and only ours. We have a sofa and a table, a clock on the wall and a Christmas biscuit tin someone gave us as decoration. I wish we had something from Syria – one fellow refugee told us she had brought her falafel moulds all the way across Europe. We don't even have a photograph of the family in Aleppo – I suppose had we known when we left four years ago that we would be separated and not return, we would have taken one, but at the time we were mainly concerned with survival.

The house is provided by the German state, which also pays the bills. They give us each 325 euros per month for adults and 180 for each child, which we use to pay for food, clothes and transport. We don't need to rely any more on Mustafa.

It's our second home in Cologne. When we were first moved from the camp in Essen on 15 October, it was to a block of refugee apartments. The apartment was on the first floor up a flight of steps which wasn't very easy for me and we had to share it with an Algerian family – a widow, her daughter and a grandchild. We had two bedrooms and they had two bedrooms, but we shared the bathroom and kitchen. We were each given a mattress, blanket, cooking pot, dish, knife, fork and spoon. The apartment was heated by a coal fire which didn't work well, so it was very cold and bad for my asthma.

The biggest problem, however, was that the woman's husband who was Syrian had just died and lots of her Algerian relatives came from France for the funeral. Six adults and four kids came to stay and every day there was a stream of visitors who had to be fed. It was crazy, and it was impossible for us to get into the kitchen. We had to ask Bland to bring us food.

After a week we went to Social Services and told them we couldn't stay there. Eventually they found us this house on a broad street of German families. We don't know our neighbours. For us Germany is a cold place – people don't go into each other's houses the way we do back home. They don't appreciate family ties like we do. I'd seen in movies how children leave their parents behind, so I knew, but to see it in real life is strange for us.

Germany is very funny. The people are like machines – they get up at a certain time, eat at a certain time and get very stressed if a train is two minutes late. We laugh at their discipline, but we like the fact that everything is very correct, not like Syria where getting a good job depends on knowing someone high up in the regime. Here everyone pays their taxes, everything is so clean and everyone seems so hard working – that's why Germany produces so much.

Bland even likes the weather, particularly the rain. I like the way there are seasons, different colours of leaves and different clouds. Occasionally, I miss the stars we used to watch from our roof in Manbij. Most of all we all like the fact we are safe. The biggest challenge is language. Nahda says it is hard for her at thirty-four to learn a new language. She is sad that her law degree, which was so hard won as the first woman in our family to go to university, is now worthless, but she is happy to see her children going to school without fear.

I miss flatbread and still find it odd that everyone eats with a knife and fork instead of their hands. I miss the familiarity of Syria – here I'm not familiar with anything and always worry that some of my behaviour might give the wrong impression even though it is normal in my country.

There is only one black cloud over our new home – the people upstairs don't like us. They are a middle-aged German couple with a grown-up son and as soon as we moved in they complained to Social Services: why do we have refugees downstairs? Once Nahda's children were playing and the woman came out screaming like a baddie from a movie and called the police. We were scared that maybe we would be taken away, so we try to be very quiet and stop the children from making any noise so she won't complain. Even so, she still shouts at us a lot.

We were shocked that somebody would have a problem with us – we are just a group of young women and little girls and my sisters always keep everything spotlessly clean. We wear jeans and shirts, not some kind of Daesh hijab. I guess she has a problem with refugees, not with us in particular. I hadn't really thought about what it meant to be a refugee, that you have no rights, and that people might be intimidated and look at you as aliens or as people with no lives who kill each other, not realizing that we do the same as them – get up in the morning, brush our teeth and go to school or work.

We had only just moved out of the camp when there was shocking news. On Saturday 18 October a politician called Henriette Reker, who was running for mayor of Cologne, was stabbed in the neck while she was out campaigning. She had been handing out roses at a market when a man came forward with a rose, pulled out a 12-inch knife and thrust it in her neck, severing her windpipe and leaving her bleeding on the ground.

The man was a forty-four-year-old unemployed handyman called Frank S. and he was angry about immigration. Frau Reker had been the head of refugee services in Cologne for the last five years and was very supportive of our plight, calling for social integration as more and more of us arrived in the city – 10,000 in the last year and 200–300 more arriving on trains every day. 'This serves you right!' the man shouted as she fell to the ground. Then he slashed four of her staff, shouting, 'Foreigners are taking our jobs.'

We were horrified that this kind lady should be attacked for standing up for refugees – striking down politicians seemed more like the sort of thing that happened in our country. That night we all prayed for her. Frau Reker was in a coma in hospital when the election took place the next day. She won with more than 52 per cent of the vote. Thank God she recovered and became Cologne's first female mayor.

As for Frank S., it turned out he had long been involved in neo-Nazi movements and had already spent three years in jail for assault. He had even participated in a demonstration in honour of Hitler's deputy Rudolf Hess, who committed suicide in prison in 1987.

Fortunately, most Germans are not like that. On the contrary they are very welcoming, almost like they want to make up for the Second World War. One day we went on an outing by bus to the nearby town of Brühl where there is a big yellow palace with ornamental gardens with so many fountains and a lake. As we walked round the lake, people smiled and even the ducks seemed to welcome us. At Christmas two people knocked on our door bearing a lot of gifts for each of us kids, including me. I was glad to still be considered a kid. And another day Nasrine and I were just arriving back from a doctor appointment and met one of our neighbours from along the street. He handed her a bag – it was full of chocolate.

Less than two weeks after we moved into the house, Shiar came over and we watched football on his laptop just as we used to. The match was France vs Germany in Paris and we supported Germany as our new country against our old occupier, but unfortunately they lost 2–0. We were chatting after the game when suddenly we noticed that all the spectators were gathering on the pitch. At first we thought they were celebrating, but then we listened to the commentary. There had been a terror attack – three suicide bombers had blown themselves up outside the stadium – so police were keeping everyone inside. The players even ended up sleeping there.

Then we heard there was shooting in bars and restaurants where people were enjoying a night out and inside a theatre called the Bataclan where lots of young people were listening to an American heavy-metal band. In total that night 130 people were killed.

Not long afterwards Daesh issued a statement claiming responsibility. 'Let France and all nations following its path know that they will continue to be at the top of the target list for the Islamic State and that the scent of death will not leave their nostrils as long as they partake in the crusader campaign … and boast about their war against Islam in France, and their strikes against Muslims in the lands of the Caliphate with their jets.'

'This is just the beginning of the storm,' it warned.

We were all very upset. Of course we had never been to Paris, but everyone knows it as the City of Light. 'This world has gone crazy,' said Nasrine. 'One of the most beautiful cities in the world being turned into a funeral is very sad. What kind of people think that because people in Syria are dying that people in Paris should too?'

Soon the attacks were linked to the refugee crisis because a Syrian passport was found near one of the suicide bombers who blew himself up outside the football stadium. It was in the name of Ahmad al-Mohammad, a twenty-five-year-old from Idlib, and Greek officials said the bomber's fingerprints matched a set taken in October when a person with that passport entered the Greek island of Leros from Turkey. Like us, the man later entered Serbia, where authorities took fingerprints matching those taken in Greece. The following day he crossed into Croatia, according to a Serbian security official.

The French Prime Minister said, 'These individuals took advantage of the refugee crisis … of the chaos, perhaps, for some of them to slip in' to France. Another of the bombers, Najim Laachroui, had been fighting with Daesh in Syria and travelled out hidden among refugees in early September to Budapest, where he was picked up by another bomber.

It was horrible to think that maybe people travelling among us, along the paths through the sunflowers and on the buses and trains, had been terrorists. Though, as Bland said, it seemed odd to take a passport to blow yourself up, and on our journey we had seen plenty of smugglers selling fake ones.

We were very worried that people would think refugees were terrorists and be scared of us. We are running from terrorism ourselves, just looking for safety because these sort of attacks are happening in our own country. We don't want to harm anyone.

After the attacks there were some demonstrations against migrants. Germany started reviewing Syrian asylum claims rather than broadly accepting them as they had been all year. That was not good for us as we were still waiting for our interviews. Some people even set fire to refugee shelters – over 800 were attacked in 2015. But generally the Germans were still open and friendly, as they had been ever since we arrived. Maybe it's easier for me being in a wheelchair as I look benign.

When I heard about such things as the Paris attacks I was glad we had no TV. There are lots of bad things going on in the world and I don't want to watch. This is an old Nujeen principle: if you want to stay happy and healthy, don't watch the news.

19

A Schoolgirl at Last

Cologne, 30 November 2015

The first day I ever went to school I was just one month shy of my seventeenth birthday. I was nervous but also happy, for finally I could say I have done something normal in my life. Of course it wasn't like in my dreams, where I thought I'd look like a girl in an American movie, walking along carrying my books, hair swinging and chatting with friends about boyfriends or movies.

In those dreams maybe after school we'd go to an ice-cream bar and I'd ask my friends if they knew the story of the Pharaoh and the Sphinx. If they said no, I would tell them how the Egyptian prince Thutmose had gone hunting for gazelle in the desert near the Pyramids and lay down in the heat of the day for a rest under the shade of the Sphinx. While he was sleeping he had a vision in which the Sphinx appeared and told him, 'If you clear all the sand that is burying me you will become king.' So he did and became Pharaoh Thutmose instead of any of his brothers, and to this day the whole story is inscribed on a pink granite slab between the Sphinx's paws. I would be like the smart girl, the nerdy girl in the group. That's what I imagine. Then I look down and see I am surrounded by these wheels and it's back to reality. Yes, I am in a wheelchair and my school is a special school, not something out of *High School Musical*.

A bus comes and picks me up at seven o'clock every morning to take me to the LVR-Christophorusschule in Bonn, which runs from 8 a.m. to 3.30 p.m. The school is a big cream two-storey building with green panels in the front and a concrete roof terrace, and as you enter, instead of bikes and scooters, there are piles of wheelchairs and walkers. There are also two football tables which one day I want to play.

I am in a class of ten fifteen-year-olds, so I am the oldest in the class and feel like an old woman. They are mostly Germans, but one girl was born in America, another boy has an American father and an English mother, and one is Jordanian. All have different ways of being 'special', some have no physical problems but are autistic, a couple don't speak and use iPads to communicate like Stephen Hawking, though they are not as smart! One just has red and yellow buttons to push which play recorded messages to indicate what she wants.

That first day was hard as of course I hardly spoke any German. Luckily the first lesson I was taken to was English, so I looked like a master. Then we cooked a pie and some kind of biscuit, which was odd for me as I had never cooked. I am not good with my hands, so I made quite a mess.

We have three teachers for my class, and they teach us German, maths, history, English and science. To start with I had a lot of difficulty. In maths I couldn't keep my work on the lines in the exercise book and I'd never done things like multiplication. The teachers and other pupils were astonished that I had never done it before, but I am a fast learner and I just do the only thing that I am good at which is listening, listening, listening. When I get frustrated because I can't do something, I reassure myself that a lot of famous people were refugees – Albert Einstein, Madeleine Albright, Gloria Estefan, George Soros. Even Steve Jobs was the son of a Syrian refugee.

We have sports like swimming which I don't do, and we break for lunch. But of course I don't like school food, so Nasrine gets up at 6 a.m. to prepare me a flask of tea and a sandwich. The teachers complain that I don't socialize, but I want to spend the time learning and, as I tell them, I am not really a social person. All my life I just stayed in a circle I felt comfortable with and grew up among adults. It's not that I don't like the other children. There is a sweet girl called Lily and others I like called Carmen and Amber. But they have different interests – the others talk about Justin Bieber and movies like *Frozen*, not like *Gone with the Wind*.

I like biology because it helps with learning everything about the body in case I get sick and need to go to the doctor.

And of course physics because of wanting to be an astronaut, though the first time I did it I came home and cried because it didn't seem like the physics of someone who was going to be a great scientist. Instead of learning about space or gravity, we were making Christmas trees on a wooden board. Even worse, because of my weak limbs and awkward fingers, I couldn't hold the board still to screw in the tree. It looked kind of ridiculous and when I took it home Nahda's kids broke it apart.

The point of this school is to train us to be as independent as possible, and when we finish here at eighteen, we do training in what they call vocational work. We have no facilities like this in Syria and I know I am very lucky – even some people in Germany think that special schools like this are too costly and that disabled people should go to school with everyone else. Maybe one day I will. I know that I didn't confront my disability in Syria because I didn't go out and so avoided people looking at me. The teachers here think I need to be realistic and accept how I am and get on with it, learn to eat by myself and move my chair, not keep talking about being an astronaut or walking. But I can't get out of my head once seeing Nasrine sitting in my wheelchair when we were in a park in Turkey and how ugly I thought that looked.

And after the soap opera that happened to my life, I think everything is possible.

*　　*　　*

A Schoolgirl at Last

At the school I go to a physiotherapist who is very nice, but she was shocked I had not done any exercises for so many years. I explained about the asthma and the revolution and the war which stopped everything. She gets me to stretch on a mat to be more flexible and to use a kind of bicycle to build up my muscles. Already I am feeling a difference.

Just after I started school I went to a hospital in Bonn for tests. That's the first time I learnt the proper name of what I have wrong with me – tetra-spasticity. The bad news is that the doctor explained that it won't go away and I will have to learn to live with it. He said I will have to have another oper-ation and prescribed me special pills to reduce my overactive legs – somehow the pills stop the charge from my brain to my nerves which make everything stiff and my legs go up in the air. I am lucky because I only have Stage One. If I had Stage Two, Three or Four like some of the children in my school, I wouldn't be able to hold a pen.

The school also sent me to an ophthalmologist and a dentist. 'There's a lot to be fixed!' I told them.

Nasrine came to my school one day and she pointed out that some of my classmates are much more disabled than me yet much more independent. They can move around on their own, get their own drinks and meals, not waiting for a sister. So now I am trying to be more independent. For the first time I get dressed myself and brush my own hair, though

Nasrine still has to get up early to get me ready in the mornings. I still dream that one day Nasrine will get married and have kids, and I go to college and she help me with physics.

I can't imagine anyone marrying someone who can't stand up. I do think I have the ability to love someone and have this image of being a mum, but am scared to think about these things. In our society we don't have that movie kind of love. Marriage is something my mum should arrange but whenever I talk about it with her Ayee immediately says 'Stop'. Maybe I will turn fully into a German and follow their way of marriage. Anyway, for now I'm too young and have a lot of other things to think about.

I feel like I missed a lot. I mean I am only now going to school, so if I go to college I will be thirty when I finish. The main thing is I finally got the normal life I dreamt of, waking in the morning, going to school, then doing homework. I just wish Ayee and Yaba could come and see me doing these things, waking up early, going to school with my pink and blue rucksack full of red subject folders.

20

A Scary New Year

Cologne, 1 January 2016

Today I turned seventeen, my first birthday in our new country. We didn't celebrate – I haven't celebrated my birthday since the war started and we left Aleppo. But there was a surprise. A package arrived with a present from James, the actor who played EJ, a silver necklace with a sea-goat, the symbol of my star sign Capricorn. Nasrine couldn't believe it.

It turned out not to be a good day. What we didn't know till later was that the night before, New Year's Eve, something terrible had happened. Just like our Newroz back home, the Germans welcome in the New Year with fireworks and parties. In Cologne they usually gather round the cathedral. That night, in the square next to the station, more than 600 women were attacked, many of them sexually assaulted.

Gangs of drunken men with 'large bloodshot eyes' had rampaged through the crowds, sexually assaulting young women, stealing their money and phones. Some had their knickers torn off or firecrackers thrown in their clothes.

The police tried to suppress news of what had happened, maybe from fear of fuelling tensions, and it took a few days for the reports to come out. When they did there was mass hysteria because Ralf Jäger, the Interior Minister for the state, said the attackers were 'exclusively' people from 'a migrant background'. People were shocked, and the opposition said that's what happens when you let too many in. An organization named Pegida, which stands for Patriotic Europeans against the Islamization of the West, called for refugees to go, shouting, 'Germany for Germans!'

We didn't know what to think. We couldn't imagine Syrian men we know ever doing such a thing. As Nasrine says, 'The problem is there are good refugees and bad refugees, just as there are well-educated people who judge people on who they are, not where they are from, and ill-educated people who don't.' Our culture is different and maybe some Muslim men, because they see German girls very scantily clad or they hear about girls getting pregnant without being married, get the wrong idea of how to behave. But molestation is bad anywhere.

One group of Syrian and Pakistani refugees were so upset they wrote to Angela Merkel to say, 'We strive to uphold the dignity and honour of women. We respect the laws of our host country without question. We are happy to have been given protection in Germany.' Anyway it didn't take long for a lynch mob to descend on the area and attack migrants. Two Pakistani men were badly beaten, as well as three Guineans and two Syrians. There were also demonstrations where people held placards proclaiming 'Rape Refugees Not Welcome – Stay Away!'

It turned out there had been similar attacks on New Year's Eve in Hamburg and other cities and the mood was changing. Around the country there were more arson attacks on shelters, and the Central Council for Muslims, which is the main Muslim group in Germany, got so many abusive calls that it was forced to disconnect its phone lines. The Council's President Almin Mazjek said, 'We are experiencing a new dimension of hatred … the far right sees its prejudices confirmed and an opportunity to give free rein to hatred of Muslims and foreigners.'

We were scared even more than after the Paris attacks because this was here, where we were living. We feared that the attacks and the anger they had stirred up might have long-term consequences, that the German opposition would say, 'Oh God, what have you done, Mrs Merkel? You have brought these weird plants to our soil,' and she might feel regret and change her mind. Less than half of Germans supported her stance, and I don't believe politicians ever do something without putting their own interests first. This is the real world and I wish I lived in a better one.

We started to worry that we would be kicked out, and we didn't know where to run. People will become aggressive, we thought, it's going to get worse and we need to be ready. We expected lots of protesting and people saying, 'Close the door.'

'We have to be ambassadors for our country and refugees,' I told Nasrine.

The police in Cologne arrested fifty-eight people. But in February a report by the local public prosecutor Ulrich Bremer said that only three of the arrested men were refugees – two Syrians and one Iraqi. The others were North African immigrants who had lived in the country a long time, and three were Germans.

Now there are police and public order vans outside the cathedral every night as a reminder of that terrible New Year's Eve. Thank God Mrs Merkel continued to resist demands to close the borders to migrants. And refugees kept coming.

A total of 91,700 entered Germany in January 2016 – about 3,000 a day, less than a third of the peak when we came the previous autumn but still more than what government officials say they can handle. In 2015, Germany registered 1.1 million requests for asylum, more than five times the number in 2014. The biggest category were Syrians.

One of them was my third sister Nahra, the fashion-loving one, who taught me to read. She came the same way as us, crossing the sea with her husband and their seven-month-old baby. It should have been harder going later, but the sea was so calm when they crossed that she filmed it on her phone!

21

A Place Called Home

Cologne, July 2016

The other day I wrote a list of all the kings and queens of England since 1066 – I counted thirty-nine.

I'd like one day to go to England to see their castles and also the Tower of London because I heard about the young princes locked in it who disappeared, maybe murdered, like something Assad would do. I'd also like to go to New York and see the Empire State Building and to St Petersburg to see the Winter Palace where the Romanovs lived and held their grand balls.

None of these things seem impossible any more. I've just been on my first ever school trip. We stayed two nights in a youth hostel in a park called Panarbora, an hour's drive from Cologne, surrounded by forest and nature as far as you could see. It rained of course, so everything was very soggy.

In the daytime the teachers took us out and told us the names of plants and trees and birds. They also wheeled us to the top of a big observation tower above the treetops, but all we could see was fog. Back in the hostel we played games like the Challenge – when it was my turn, I said I would name ten capital cities in a minute and a half while drinking hot chocolate. One of my classmates who is very slow at doing things said she would paint one of us and at the end we had to guess who it was – it turned out to be me!

Then we did a Compliments Shower, where we got in a semi-circle and took turns to go in front and everyone had to write on a card what they liked about that person. In my case they said I spoke German well, was a genius at learning languages, had a nice smile and was funny and loving.

I always wanted to have these memories of a school trip. They came late in my childhood but better late than never. I shared a room with three other girls from my class. Only one could walk. But I started to realize it didn't matter. It was the first time I had ever slept in a place without anyone looking after me and that was a good feeling. The first night, though, I nearly cried because we had a camp fire and were given special German breads on sticks to grill, but I didn't know how to and kept burning them. I hate to feel foolish or foreign, and of course when they started singing I didn't know any of the German songs.

When the bus dropped me back at Wesseling, my family asked, 'Didn't you miss us?' I realized that actually I hadn't because I was too busy with everything being new. The saddest thing was at the end of the trip when the teachers said we are going home. I thought what is home? There is no going back to my country.

Of course I never forget Syria. Now we have TV and an iPad sent by fans of *Days of Our Lives*, and every day we watch events back home on the news or Facebook. One day someone posted film from our street in Aleppo, George al-Aswad, everything destroyed like a scene from Dresden, apart from our building, still standing as it was when my parents went back. Sometimes, as I watch yet more bombing, yet more innocent people fleeing, the war feels as if it's in some far-off land, nothing to do with me.

It might not have seemed possible, but everything there has got even more complicated. Shortly after we arrived in Germany, the Russians – who had been backing Assad all along – got more involved in our war, sending their air force and starting airstrikes, sometimes as many as sixty a day. They said they were attacking Daesh but mostly they seemed to be targeting rebels, and also hospitals. They got Homs back for Assad, which looks like a ghost town, and drove Daesh from the ancient city of Palmyra, then sent in a symphony orchestra to play a weird kind of victory concert amid the ruins. Now the town is under Russian control.

Assad has launched a massive assault on Aleppo to take control, even if he turns it into dust, and is choking off all the roads in and out. That's not all. He dropped so many barrel bombs on the town of Daraya near Damascus the day after the United Nations and Red Cross delivered the first food aid to starving people for more than three years that a UN official recently described the town as 'Syria's capital of barrel bombing'.

'There is something fundamentally wrong in a world where attacks on hospitals and schools … have become so commonplace that they cease to incite any reaction,' said Stephen O'Brien, UN Under-Secretary-General for Humanitarian Affairs. He told the Security Council, 'The real measure [of success] will be when these medieval sieges are no more, when boys don't risk sniper fire when bringing medicine to their mothers, when doctors can administer life-saving treatments without the fear of imminent attacks, when Yazidi girls don't have to scratch their faces out of fear of being bought and sexually enslaved. That is the disgusting reality in Syria today.'

Yet Western politicians have started saying 'better the devil you know' about Assad, and it seems like the world has just accepted him after all the talk of his barbarity and him crossing red lines. The West only seems to care about Daesh because they have attracted so many of its young to fight and then return home and launch attacks on Western cities like Paris and Brussels. It keeps bombing them in Iraq and Syria and people say Daesh have lost a lot of their territory and many of their leaders and are preparing for the end of the Caliphate.

As for Manbij, after two years of Daesh control we hear it has been mostly taken back by our Kurdish YPG, working with some of the local Arab sheikhs and helped by US airstrikes. Unfortunately we hear some of the strikes killed dozens of civilians, including children. Around 45,000 fled but thousands of people are trapped inside without food. Manbij is a key supply stop for Daesh en route to their capital Raqqa, so losing it would be a big deal. The YPG, by the way, helped by the US, are responsible for almost all the territorial gains from Daesh in northern Syria, which makes us hopeful we will get our Kurdistan. But people are worried because President Erdoğan sent his Turkish warplanes to hit targets over the border. 'Manbij does not belong to Kurds; it is a place where Arabs live,' he said. 'If needed we will take matters into our own hands.'

We Skype every day with my parents back in Gaziantep. Yaba is sad. 'I think my country is lost,' he says. 'Everywhere is fighting. I left behind my fields and my children don't pray.' He always complains we don't pray, which is not true. I'm more religious than I look and was raised in a country where religious belief is very strict. My sisters are all fasting for Ramadan. But one thing I haven't told him. My school sometimes takes us to church. I like the music, it's awesome, but I don't sing with the others in case I accidentally sing something that's like a Bible verse. Everything in Islam has consequences. Going to church during Ramadan – what an irony!

I am settling into school, speaking German and have even made friends who sometimes appear in my dreams instead of the bombings, though the teachers still complain I don't socialize. The school arranged a new wheelchair for me which is blue, my favourite colour, and not so wide like the last one which I just sank into. The main thing is it's much lighter and I can manoeuvre it myself, even up and down kerbs, and I have even started playing wheelchair basketball.

Nasrine is now doing German classes every afternoon, so maybe I will lose my job as family translator. I don't mind so much any more as I think maybe I can have other uses.

Now we have a TV at home we all get together and watch football like the old days, even ordering in my favourite pizza. If it's Barcelona and they lose, particularly to Real Madrid, I shout at Nasrine, 'Get out, I don't want to talk to you!' She doesn't like that, but I'm glad that despite everything I am still a normal teenager who can scream if Barcelona lose and that my spirit wasn't killed. We supported our new country Germany in the Euros and were sad when they lost in the semi-finals.

One day we went to Cologne Zoo and saw lots of the animals I have seen in documentaries like crimson flamingos, giraffes with no vocal cords and piranhas that can strip the flesh off someone in ninety seconds. A bird with a kind of skirt of colourful feathers came to look at my wheelchair as if we were both weird creatures. While we were there we met some Kurds – we Kurds always recognize each other!

Now we are settled I have a long list of people I want to look up and investigate – Margaret Thatcher, Steve Jobs, Bill Gates, also Einstein – was he a crazy man or a genius? I would also like to go back to the Alps in Austria and find the castle where there is a portrait of the real-life Beauty and the Beast – the story which had been my favourite as a child. Back in Aleppo I once watched a documentary called *The Real Beauty and the Beast* about a man called Petrus Gonsalvus, born in Tenerife in the sixteenth century covered in hair from head to toe like a wolf. He was suffering from a rare condition called hypertrichosis which only affects men and there are fifty people with it in the world today. Petrus was taken from his home as a boy and given to King Henri II of France, and the queen Catherine de Médici had him married to a beautiful woman who didn't know what he looked like. But she stayed with him and they had seven children so she must have loved his inner beauty. They were taken on a tour of European courts like curiosities and were painted. But when they had children the ones who inherited the condition were taken from them and given away to European nobles like pets.

* * *

Nujeen

Speaking of curiosities, in June 2016 I was invited with a group of refugees to go to Berlin to meet a lady called Samantha Power, the American Ambassador to the United Nations. I went on the train with Nasrine and we laughed at how it's become just normal for us to take trains. I was excited to see this famous city where until the year Nasrine was born there was a wall dividing it and where Hitler and Eva Braun killed themselves in the bunker.

There were about a dozen refugees and everyone told their stories, which were heartbreaking, and I wished I didn't have to listen. But they also showed how they were trying to make a positive contribution to life in their new country.

There was a doctor called Hamber who had been a political prisoner in Damascus and was trying to get accredited to practise medicine in Germany. In the meantime he has been volunteering as an interpreter for refugees undergoing medical examinations in Berlin.

There was also a young man called Bourak from Aleppo like us. He had been at the university like Nasrine, studying computer science, and of course, like her, his studies had been brought to an end. He was learning German and was desperate to go back to university and has designed an app called BureauCrazy to help asylum seekers navigate the application process and make the forms available in multiple languages.

Ambassadors don't have much time and we didn't get long to speak. When it was my turn I told her, 'We are just people who are dying every day for the chance to brush their teeth in the morning and go to school.' I also said to her, 'Everyone wants to speak to me because I am smiling – is it so rare to find a smiling refugee? Am I like an alien?'

Bland, Nasrine and Nahda have all been granted asylum after going to a court in Düsseldorf and answering questions, and they have their residency papers. But I am still waiting, maybe as I am a minor. In my case instead of going to court I had an interview with my German guardian. She asked me about the journey and why I left Syria, if I had seen horrific things and whether I had any proof of the difficulties in my homeland. Nasrine and I laughed afterwards – doesn't she watch the news?

Nahda has applied for family reunification and is hoping her husband Mustafa can join them. It's almost a year since they waved goodbye on the beach in Turkey. Nahra has been settled near Hamburg with her husband, waiting for asylum, and we hope to see her. Only Jamila is still in Syria, in Kobane, because her husband wouldn't leave. They have electricity now and Daesh have gone, but life is hard and there are no schools open for her children.

I know we are lucky. My cousin Evelin who travelled across Europe in the same group as Nahda is still in a camp set up in a basketball court. She says her things are stolen all the time – her phone, even her clothes when she hangs them up – and she has the same three pieces of bread, butter and jam for breakfast every morning. They queue for hours to collect pocket money. We also hear from friends in Berlin that they are scared to go out because of hostility. Some even want to go back to Turkey or Syria, but now it's impossible. My brother Mustafa and his wife Dozgeen applied to go to America through UNHCR in Turkey a year ago but are still waiting for an interview date.

No one is doing the journey we did any more. As Germany changed its mind about accepting refugees after the Cologne attacks, in March the European Union signed a deal with Turkey to pay them 6 billion euros to close their borders and coastline and stop the flow of migrants. Mustafa says there is lots of barbed wire now and Turkish military in tanks at Jarablus. A whole lot of people got stuck in Greece when the borders closed. More than 50,000 are still there, including in the camps on Lesbos, and some of our cousins who were at Idomeni, trying to get into Macedonia when Europe shut its doors.

The only options now for those leaving Syria are Lebanon, which is stretched to the limit as one in five of the population are Syrian, and Jordan, which has 1.3 million Syrian refugees on top of its own population of 6.5 million and recently closed its crossing, leaving thousands stranded in the desert at the border. Our own journey here seems long ago. Though it was born from tragedy, I remember it as the biggest adventure in my life, a story to tell my grandchildren.

Recently some fans of *Days of Our Lives* who had heard my story came to meet us with amazing gifts like blue headphones and the iPad and took me and Nasrine for a trip on a boat on the Rhine. To my surprise I realized Nasrine was crying. She told me she was remembering the boat to Greece. 'It was all right for you, you didn't have the responsibility,' she said.

The tiniest particle in the universe is a quark and that's what I feel like in this big mass of migrants. Around 5 million of my countrymen have left Syria since the war started in 2011 and 1.1 million of them made the journey like us across Europe. Around 430,000 came to Germany. One-quarter of the total refugees are children like me aged seventeen or under.

We don't have a lot of choice. Of those who stayed in Syria, more than 250,000 have been killed. Some have been under siege so long they haven't seen the moon for two years. In Germany they call us *Flüchtlinge*. Nasrine says it sounds like a bird, but I hate that word, just as I hate refugee and migrant. They're totally harsh.

Recently the trial took place of Frank S., the man who tried to kill Frau Reker, the mayor of Cologne. He complained that Germany was heading for 'self-destruction' by accepting so many refugees. 'I saw it as a final opportunity to change something,' he told the court. He'd even told one police officer after his arrest that he also wanted to kill Mrs Merkel. He was convicted of attempted murder and sentenced to fourteen years in prison. 'He wanted to send a signal to the federal government about refugee policy,' said the judge, Barbara Havliza. 'He wanted to create a climate of fear, and influence policy.'

Then, in the third week of July, when school had finished and everyone was getting into the holiday mood, Germany suddenly had seven days of terror. It started on a Monday when a seventeen-year-old refugee, initially described as an Afghan and later as a Pakistani, pulled out an axe on a train in Würzburg, wounding four passengers and a woman walking her dog, before police shot him.

Four days later in a shopping centre in Munich, an eighteen-year-old German-Iranian lured teenagers to McDonald's by promising free food and started a shooting spree, killing nine people. Two days after that came two more attacks in Bavaria. A twenty-one-year-old Syrian with a machete killed a Polish woman, while another one exploded a bomb in a backpack at the entrance to a music festival, killing himself and injuring fifteen people.

Three of the four attackers were refugees, two of them Syrian. So once again everyone is looking at refugees. One Dutch politician even said the EU should refuse entry to all Muslims. 'We have imported a monster and the monster is called Islam,' he said.

Words like that make us shudder. Actually these attackers are completely ignorant about the real spirit of Islam. But of course these attacks are making people suspicious of refugees. In some ways I am glad they blocked off the way and no one is coming any more.

We're worried how much endurance Mrs Merkel has. She has stood up so far to those who want to get rid of us but these attacks are on her citizens and, unlike in our part of the world, politicians in countries like Germany listen to their people. No one is going to care for us if we are damaging their country.

Poor Europeans, they are experiencing what we experienced. Feeling insecure is not a good thing. We still jump at bangs and at the sound of a high-pitched voice. I don't want my new home to be like that too.

The woman upstairs still doesn't talk to us. But now we have found out that it isn't just that we are refugees. It turns out that the house was actually owned by a man who had two daughters and left them each half the house when he died. One of the daughters is the woman living upstairs and she wants to buy the downstairs and have the whole house but her sister's husband won't agree and rents to us.

So here's the thing as I see it. Yes, I know we are expensive. Looking after migrants in 2015 cost German taxpayers more than $23 billion, according to the Economic Research Institute in Munich. But give us a chance and we can contribute. If you don't want to let refugees in for humanitarian reasons, what about the benefit we bring to the economy? You actually have to be quite resilient and resourceful to navigate all the way here, through all those people wanting to rob and cheat you or close off the way. Most of us who have fled are skilled or educated. I know I didn't go to school but I speak fluent soap-opera English.

Germany for example has the world's lowest birth rate and its population has been shrinking for years. By 2060 its population will have shrunk from 81 million to 67 million. To keep its industry going so it can remain Europe's largest economy it needs our foreign labour. Germany has already given asylum to 240,000 Syrians, including my brother and sisters thought not yet me. As for the European Union, that has 500 million people, so like I said before, even if they took all 1.1 million Syrians who came to Europe that would only be just over 0.2 per cent – far fewer than were taken in by countries after the Second World War that everyone keeps referring to. Some countries have accepted only small numbers. The UK has only taken 5,465, a quarter of the number accepted last year by the city of Cologne. I guess unlike Germany, the UK's population has been expanding. Prime Minister David Cameron promised to take 20,000 by 2020 but had to resign after losing a referendum where people voted to leave the EU partly because they wanted to stop migrants coming.

When you get to know us you will see we are not that different. Like I told you, the reason we don't have a family photo is we never imagined something like this would happen to us.

* * *

I wanted to go into space and find an alien, but here sometimes I feel like one.

I miss my room on the fifth floor in Aleppo watching TV. Now I have a real life. Sometimes I try to block it out by putting on my headphones, switching on the TV and taking myself back to the old days. I feel like the old Nujeen is being erased and a new one being generated. I miss my country, even the house with cats and dogs, and I miss the way the doors of our homes are always open. I miss the sound of the *azaan* – the call for prayer that used to rise up to our balcony. I heard that some refugees have even put an app with the call on their phone. I feel guilty having left my homeland.

Most of all I miss Ayee and Yaba and my sister Jamila and I fear I won't see my parents again because they are old. I worry about being left alone.

I don't miss Syria when I think how difficult my life was. When I remember how scared I was, how much danger we were in, I think Thank God we are here. Only God knows when this whole thing will be over, and the Syria we knew will never exist again. I long for the day when death will become abnormal again for me. Maybe one day we will get our Kurdistan, our Rojava. Just now I was watching a YouTube video called '10 Countries That Might Exist in the Future' and guess what was number one? Kurdistan!

And I wonder. If we ever go back, will we recognize each other? I have changed and my country has changed.

* * *

Coming to Germany was my dream. Maybe I won't be an astronaut. Maybe I will never learn to walk. But there are lots of good things in this society and I'd like to put them with good things from my society and make a Nujeen cocktail.

I go to school proud in my new yellow T-shirt that says 'Girls Love Unicorns' and my silver necklace from a soap-opera star and I can dream. And now you have read my story I hope you see I am not just a number – none of us are.

Appendix

My Journey

Total distance 3593 miles, total travel cost 5045 euros (for me and my sister)

Syria

2012

27 July   Aleppo to Manbij
                                56 miles by minibus

2014

August   Manbij to Jarablus
                                24 miles by Uncle Ahmed's car
                                $50 (46 euros) to cross border

On the same day   Jarablus to Gaziantep (Turkey)
                                107 miles by Uncle Ahmed's car

ONE YEAR ON

Turkey

2015

22 August   Gaziantep to İzmir
691 miles by plane: 300 euros each

İzmir airport to Basmane Square
18 miles by taxi: 15 euros

1 September   İzmir to Behram
156 miles by bus and taxi: 100 euros

2 September   Behram to Skala Sikamineas, Lesbos
(Greece)
8 miles by boat: $1,500 (1330 euros)
each, plus 50 euros each for life
jacket

Greece

3 September   Skala Sikamineas to Mitilini
30 miles by car (lift from volunteer)

9 September   Mitilini to Athens
Taxi from Pikpa camp to ferry:
10 euros
261 miles by ferry: 60 euros each

| 14 September | Athens to Thessaloniki |
| | 312 miles by train: 42 euros each |

| | Thessaloniki to Evzonoi |
| | 55 miles by taxi: 100 euros |

| 15 September | Evzonoi to Gevgelija (Macedonia) |
| | 1.2 miles on foot |

Macedonia

| 15 September | Gevgelija to Lojane |
| | 125 miles by taxi: 200 euros |

| | Lojane to Miratovac (Serbia) |
| | 1.9 miles on foot (or by wheelchair) |

Serbia

| 15 September | Miratovac to Belgrade |
| | 243 miles by bus: 35 euros each |

| | Belgrade to Horgoš |
| | 124 miles by taxi: 210 euros |

| 16 September | Horgoš to Röszke |
| | 7.5 miles by bus: 5 euros each |

| | Röszke to Apatin |
| | 78 miles by taxi: approx. 125 euros |

Croatia

16 September	From Apatin through fields into Croatia, then by police van to a small village (name unknown)
	Small village to Zagreb 209 miles by bus
17 September	Zagreb to Žumberački road 21 miles by taxi: 100 euros
	Žumberački road to Slovenska Vas (Slovenia) 0.6 miles on foot

Slovenia

17 September	Slovenska Vas to Perišče 2.5 miles by police van
18 September	Perišče to Postojna 100 miles by bus
20 September	Postojna to Logatec 17 miles by bus
	Logatec to Maribor 99 miles by train
	Maribor to Spielfeld (Austria) 14 miles by taxi: 5 euros

Appendix: My Journey

Austria

20 September, midnight	Spielfeld to Graz 31 miles by bus
21 September	Graz to Salzburg 173 miles by train: 60 euros each
	Salzburg to Saalach bridge 5 miles by police bus
	Saalach bridge to Rosenheim (Germany) 50 miles by bus

Germany

22 September	Rosenheim to Neumarkt 137 miles by bus
	Neumarkt to Nuremberg 27 miles by taxi: 50 euros
	Nuremberg to Cologne 267 miles by train: 115 euros each
23 September	Cologne to Dortmund (refugee centre) 59 miles by train: 45 euros each
24 September	Dortmund to Essen 30 miles by bus

15 October

Essen to Wesseling
52 miles by minibus

Acknowledgements

Thank you to my family for so whole-heartedly embracing this unexpected extra child and always showing so much patience with me.

I thank God for giving me everything I have and I pray for the story of my life to have a happy ending.

The last year has been a journey I could never have imagined back in our fifth-floor apartment in Aleppo. I have gone from the girl who never left her room and saw the world outside only through TV to crossing an entire continent using every form of transport – all that's left is a cable car, submarine and of course spaceship!

I am just one of millions of refugees, many of whom like me are children, and my journey was easier than that of many. But it wouldn't have been possible without all the kind people who helped along the way, from the old ladies and fishermen on the beach in Lesbos to the volunteers and aid-workers who gave us water and helped push me.

I can never express enough gratitude to Mrs Merkel and Germany for giving me a home and my first ever experience of school. There, I have been helped enormously by my teachers Ingo Schrot, Andrea Becker and Stefanie Vree and my physiotherapist Bogena Schmilewski. Thank you to my German guardian Ulrike Mehren for guiding me.

Thanks as well to the writers of *Days of Our Lives* who had no idea they were giving an education to a little girl in Aleppo. In particular to Melissa Salmons, who worked on the script of EJ and Sami – and for the kindness of its wonderful fans especially Giselle Rheindorf Hale.

I'm incredibly grateful to Christina for putting words to my story, and her family Paulo and Lourenço for their support (even if they do like Cristiano Ronaldo and, by the way, congratulations Portugal for winning Euro, shame it wasn't Spain!)

Thank you Fergal Keane for bringing us together! Christina would like to thank all the people who helped in her reporting of the refugee crisis, in particular Babar Baloch of UNHCR, Alison Criado-Perez of MSF and the Catrambone family. We would both also like to thank Hassan Kadoni. Thanks also to our agent David Godwin, and fabulous editor Arabella Pike and her team Joe Zigmond and Essie Cousins, fantastic copy editor Peter James, designer Julian Humphries, and to Matt Clacher and Laura Brooke for getting so much behind the book.

Above all to my sister Nasrine for pushing me all across Europe and putting up with all my information even if she didn't always listen.

Index

Index

Index

Index

Index

FOR EVERY CHILD IN DANGER

unicef

UNITED KINGDOM

UNICEF UK CAMPAIGNS TO KEEP CHILD REFUGEES SAFE.

We believe that refugee children should be with their families. No child should be alone, stuck in wretched camps or forced to risk their lives on dangerous journeys.

To find out more about our campaign and to add your voice, please visit our website

UNICEF.UK